THE CROSS
and the
SWITCHBLADE

THE CROSS
and the
SWITCHBLADE

The Greatest Inspirational True Story of All Time

DAVID WILKERSON

WITH JOHN AND ELIZABETH SHERRILL

FOREWORD BY CAMERON DANTE

ZONDERVAN™

GRAND RAPIDS, MICHIGAN 49530 USA

ZONDERVAN™

The Cross and the Switchblade
Copyright © 1963 by David Wilkerson; Foreword © 2002 Cameron Dante

Requests for information should be addressed to:

Zondervan
Grand Rapids, Michigan 49530

First published in the United States of America by Jove Publications, Inc. in 1962

First published in Great Britain by Lakeland Press in 1967

First published by Zondervan in 2002

ISBN 0-310-24829-9

Interior design by Susan Ambs

Printed in the United States of America

03 04 05 06 /❖ DC/ 12 11 10 9 8 7 6 5 4

To my wife, Gwen

Foreword

What an absolute honour! As I sat down to write the foreword for this classic, it brought back very real memories for me. *The Cross and the Switchblade* was the first book ever handed to me by a Christian. And it was the first book to show me that God is right here on the street, doing business in ordinary people's lives.

I had already begun to ask questions, and I was already searching for spiritual answers. But nobody understood me. How could they? No one had ever walked in my shoes. No one knew the difficulties I faced. Christianity reminded me of a middle-class, well-to-do, organized conspiracy. No Christian had approached me while I was in the courtroom. Not one had tried to talk to me when I was doing my gear. None had tried to help me when I was skint and didn't know where my next meal was coming from.

But all that changed when a Canadian evangelist became concerned for my welfare and gave me a copy of the book you're holding. *The Cross and the Switchblade* was just what I needed to encourage me in my new-found faith. It sorted my head out, and it showed me that God will go to incredible lengths to reach incredible nutters like me. Was I the only one with an amazing story of God's love? No! God has been transforming lives daily across the world since time began.

Nicky Cruz was somebody I could relate to. His story may have happened before I was born, yet it had the hallmark of the underground world I was living in. The gangs were the same, the struggle to survive in a world of have's and have not's was the same, the violence was the same, and the drugs were the same. Whatever caused this guy to take a serious look at God was bugging me, for his story was close enough to mine to challenge me. He fought against the truth of Jesus Christ, yet the love and consistency of one man – David Wilkerson – showed through his confusion. Would it do the same for me?

As I began reading *The Cross and the Switchblade*, I burst into tears at the turn of every page. This was not normal and I felt embarrassed – it was a good job I was on my own. I knew what Nicky Cruz was going through; I understood him and his lifestyle. But in the midst of a story centred on fighting to survive, one man stood out. David Wilkerson was the mad vicar who turned the whole story around. He was the middle-class Christian who 'done my head in.' Here was a God who had no social barriers. God could change the life of a middle-class person just as much as a lower-class bloke like me.

David Wilkerson's story caused me to look closely at the Christian faith. Why would anybody want to take risks for people like us? Why would anybody give so much of his or her time and effort for the sake of a religious idea? Here was a man who was obviously inspired by something he believed was true. 'Good for him,' I thought. I knew the old cliché, 'stand for something or fall for anything.' I'd fallen for anything and everything in my battle to be the top dog, and all it ever did was get me into more trouble.

This story had me on the edge of my seat. As I read about Nicky's battles with opposing gangs to gain their 'manor,' I could see myself. As I saw his fight to stay loyal to his mates, I saw myself. As I saw his hatred for the 'old bill,' I saw myself.

Nicky Cruz's story is still as relevant and as fresh today as the day it was printed. I dare you to see yourself. And I dare you to dream what you could be with Jesus involved in your life.

Read on. This true story gave me the inspiration to carry on. I know that when you are at your lowest, when you feel lost and unable to cope with life, and when you can't see any way out of the worst that life has thrown you, God can sort it out. How will he do it? Probably through ordinary people. If you are ready to be inspired and challenged to look at the life of Jesus Christ and his work among ordinary people, *The Cross and the Switchblade* is for you.

Cameron Dante
Radio DJ/ Promoter
Author of *Ascension: Clubs, Drugs and the Eternal High*

Chapter One

This whole strange adventure got its start late one night when I was sitting in my study reading *Life* magazine, and turned a page.

At first glance, it seemed that there was nothing on the page to interest me. It carried a pen drawing of a trial taking place in New York City, 350 miles away. I'd never been to New York, and I never wanted to go, except perhaps to see the Statue of Liberty.

I started to flip the page over. But as I did, my attention was caught by the eyes of one of the figures in the drawing. A boy. One of seven boys on trial for murder. The artist had caught such a look of bewilderment and hatred and despair in his features that I opened the magazine wide again to get a closer look. And as I did, I began to cry.

'What's the matter with me!' I said aloud, impatiently brushing away a tear. I looked at the picture more carefully. The boys were all teen-agers. They were members of a gang called the Dragons. Beneath their picture was the story of how they had gone into Highbridge Park in New York and brutally attacked and killed a fifteen-year-old polio victim named Michael Farmer. The seven boys stabbed Michael in the back seven times with their knives, then beat him over the head with garrison belts. They went away wiping blood through their hair, saying, 'We messed him good.'

The story revolted me. It turned my stomach. In our little mountain town such things seemed mercifully unbelievable.

That's why I was dumbfounded by a thought that sprang suddenly into my head – full-blown, as though it had come into me from somewhere else.

Go to New York City and help those boys.

I laughed out loud. 'Me? Go to New York? A country preacher barge into a situation he knows less than nothing about?'

Go to New York City and help those boys. The thought was still there, vivid as ever, apparently completely independent of my own feelings and ideas.

'I'd be a fool. I know nothing about kids like that. I don't want to know anything.'

It was no use. The idea would not go away: I was to go to New York, and furthermore I was to go at once, while the trial was still in progress.

In order to understand what a complete departure such an idea was for me, it is necessary first to know that until I turned that page, mine had been a very predictable life. Predictable, but satisfying. The little mountain church which I served in Philipsburg, Pennsylvania, had grown slowly but steadily. We had a new church building, a new parsonage, a swelling missionary budget. There was satisfaction for me in our growth, because four years earlier when Gwen and I first drove into Philipsburg as candidates for the empty pulpit, the church didn't even have a building of its own. The congregation of fifty members was meeting in a private house, using the upstairs as the parsonage and the downstairs for the sanctuary.

When the Pulpit Committee was showing us around, I remember, Gwen's heel went right through the 'parsonage' floor.

'Things do need fixing up a bit,' admitted one of the church women, a large lady in a cotton print dress. I remember noticing that her hands had little cracks around the knuckles and that the cracks were filled with dirt from farm work. 'We'll just leave you to look around.'

And so Gwen continued her tour of the second floor alone. I could tell by the way she was closing doors that she was unhappy. But the real blow came when she opened a kitchen drawer. I heard her scream and rushed upstairs. They were still there, scurrying about: seven or eight big fat black cockroaches.

Gwen slammed the drawer shut.

'Oh, Dave, I just couldn't!' she cried.

And without waiting for me to answer, she raced to the hall and ran down the stairs, her high heels clacking loudly. I made hurried apologies to the Committee and followed Gwen over to the hotel – the only hotel in Philipsburg – where I found her waiting for me with the baby.

'I'm sorry, honey,' Gwen said. 'They're such nice people, but I'm scared to death of cockroaches.'

She was already packed. It was obvious that as far as Gwen was concerned, Philipsburg, Pennsylvania, would have to find another candidate.

But things didn't work out that way. We couldn't go before evening because I was scheduled to preach the Sunday night service. I don't remember that it was a good sermon. Yet something about it seemed to strike the fifty people in this little house-church. Several of the rough-handed farmers, sitting there before me, were blowing into their handkerchiefs. I wound up the sermon and was mentally getting into my car and driving out through the hills away from Philipsburg when suddenly one old gentleman stood right up in the service and said,

'Reverend Wilkerson, will you come and be our pastor?'

It was a rather unorthodox thing to do, and it caught everyone by surprise, including my wife and me. The people in this small Assembly of God church had been trying to choose between several candidates. They had been dead-locked for weeks, and now old Mr Meyer was taking matters into his own hands and inviting me from the floor. But instead of drawing fire, he found himself surrounded by nodding heads and voices of approval.

'You go outside for a minute and talk it over with your wife,' Mr Meyer said. 'We'll join you.'

Outside in the dark car, Gwen was silent. Debbie was asleep in her wicker basket in the back seat, our suitcase was propped up next to her, packed and ready to go. And in Gwen's silence was a quiet protest against cockroaches.

'We need help, Gwen,' I said hurriedly. 'I think we should pray.'

'Ask Him about those roaches,' Gwen said darkly.

'All right, I'll do just that.'

I bowed my head. There in the dark outside that little church I made an experiment in a special kind of prayer which seeks to find God's will through a sign. 'Putting a fleece before the Lord,' it is called, because Gideon, when he was trying to find God's will for his life, asked that a sign be made with a fleece. He placed a lamb's fleece on the ground and asked Him to send down dew everywhere but there. In the morning, the ground was soaked with dew, but Gideon's fleece was dry: God had granted him a sign.

'Lord,' I said aloud, 'I would like to put a fleece before You now. Here we are ready to do Your will if we can just find out what it is. Lord, if You want us to stay here in Philipsburg, we ask that You let us know by having the Committee vote for us unanimously. And let them decide of their own accord to fix up the parsonage with a decent refrigerator and stove ...'

'And Lord,' said Gwen, interrupting because just then the front door of the church opened and the Committee started toward us, 'let them volunteer to get rid of those cockroaches.'

The whole congregation followed the Committee outside and gathered around the car where Gwen and I now stood. Mr Meyer cleared his throat. As he spoke, Gwen squeezed my hand in the dark.

'Reverend and Mrs Wilkerson,' he said. He paused and commenced again. 'Brother David. Sister Gwen. We've taken a vote and everyone agrees that we want you to be our new pastor.

Hundred per cent. If you decide to come, we'll fix up the parsonage with a new stove and things, and Sister Williams says we'll have to fumigate the place.'

'To get rid of those cockroaches,' added Mrs Williams, addressing herself to Gwen.

In the light that streamed over the lawn from the open front door of the church, I could see that Gwen was crying. Later, back in the hotel, after we'd finished with handshaking all around, Gwen said that she was very happy.

———————

And we *were* happy in Philipsburg. The life of a country preacher suited me perfectly. Most of our parishioners were either farmers or coal workers, honest, God-fearing and generous. They brought in tithes of canned goods, butter, eggs, milk and meat. They were creative, happy people, people you could admire and learn from.

After I'd been there a little more than a year, we purchased an old baseball lot on the edge of town, where Lou Gehrig had once played ball. I remember the day I stood on home plate, looked out toward the infield, and asked the Lord to build us a church right there with the cornerstone on home plate and the pulpit at shortstop. And that's what happened, too.

We built a parsonage next door to the church, and as long as Gwen was mistress of that house, no vermin had a chance. It was a pretty little five-room pink bungalow with a view of the hills out one side and the white cross of the church out the other.

Gwen and I worked hard in Philipsburg, and we had a certain kind of success. By New Year's Day, 1958, there were 250 people in the parish – including Bonnie, a new little daughter of our own.

And I was restless. I was beginning to feel a kind of spiritual discontent that wasn't satisfied by looking at the new church building on its five acres of hilltop land, or the swelling missionary budget, or the crowding in the pews. I remember the precise night on which I recognized it, as people do remember important dates in their lives. It was February 9, 1958. On that night I decided to sell my television set.

It was late, Gwen and the children were asleep, and I was sitting in front of the set watching the 'Late Show'. The story somehow involved a dance routine in which a lot of chorus girls marched across the set in just-visible costumes. I remember thinking suddenly how dull it all was.

'You're getting old, David,' I warned myself.

But try as I would, I could not get my mind back on the threadbare little story and the girl – which one was it? – whose destiny on the stage was supposed to be a matter of palpitating interest to every viewer.

I got up and turned the knob and watched the young girls disappear into a little dot in the center of the screen. I left the living room and went into my office and sat down in the brown leather swivel chair.

'How much time do I spend in front of that screen each night?' I wondered. 'A couple of hours, at least. What would happen, Lord, if I sold that TV set and spent that time – praying?' I was the only one in the family who ever watched TV anyway.

What would happen if I spent two hours every single night in prayer? It was an exhilarating idea. Substitute prayer for television, and see what happened.

Right away I thought of objections to the idea. I was tired at night. I needed the relaxation and change of pace. Television was part of our culture; it wasn't good for a minister to be out of touch with what people were seeing and talking about.

I got up from my chair and turned out the lights and stood at my window looking out over the moonlit hills. Then I put another fleece before the Lord, one which was destined to change my life. I made it pretty hard on God, it seemed to me, because I really didn't want to give up television.

'Jesus,' I said, 'I need some help deciding this thing, so here's what I'm asking of You. I'm going to put an ad for that set in the paper. If You're behind this idea, let a buyer appear right away. Let him appear within an hour ... within half an hour ... after the paper gets on the streets.'

When I told Gwen about my decision next morning, she was unimpressed. 'Half an hour!' she said. 'Sounds to me, Dave Wilkerson, like you don't want to do all that praying.'

Gwen had a point, but I put the ad in the paper anyhow. It was a comical scene in our living room after the paper appeared. I sat on the sofa with the television set looking at me from one side, the children and Gwen looking at me from another, and my eyes on a great big alarm clock beside the telephone.

Twenty-nine minutes passed by the clock.

'Well, Gwen,' I said, 'it looks like you're right. I guess I won't have to ...'

The telephone rang.

I picked it up slowly, looking at Gwen.

'You have a TV set for sale?' a man's voice asked.

'That's right. An RCA in good condition. Nineteen-inch screen, two years old.'

'How much to you want for it?'

'One hundred dollars,' I said quickly. I hadn't thought about what to ask for it until that moment.

'I'll take it,' the man said, just like that.

'You don't even want to look at it?'

'No. Have it ready in fifteen minutes. I'll bring the money.'

———————

My life has not been the same since. Every night at midnight, instead of flipping some dials, I stepped into my office, closed the door, and began to pray. At first the time seemed to drag and I grew restless. Then I learned how to make systematic Bible-reading a part of my prayer life: I'd never before read the

Bible through, including all the begats. And I learned how important it is to strike a balance between prayer of petition and prayer of praise. What a wonderful thing it is to spend a solid hour just being thankful. It throws all of life into a new perspective.

It was during one of these late evenings of prayer that I picked up *Life* magazine.

I'd been strangely fidgety all night. I was alone in the house; Gwen and the children were in Pittsburgh visiting grandparents. I had been at prayer for a long time. I felt particularly close to God, and yet for reasons I could not understand I also felt a great, heavy sadness. It came over me all at once and I wondered what it could possibly mean. I got up and turned on the lights in the study. I felt uneasy, as though I had received orders but could not make out what they were.

'What are you saying to me, Lord?'

I walked around the study, seeking to understand what was happening to me. On my desk lay a copy of *Life*. I reached over and started to pick it up, then caught myself. No, I wasn't going to fall into that trap: reading a magazine when I was supposed to be praying.

I started prowling around the office again and each time I came to the desk my attention was drawn to that magazine.

'Lord, is there something in there You want me to see?' I said aloud, my voice suddenly booming out in the silent house.

I sat down in my brown leather swivel chair and with a pounding heart, as if I were on the verge of something bigger than I could understand, I opened the magazine. A moment later I was looking at a pen drawing of seven boys, and tears were streaming down my face.

The next night was Wednesday prayer meeting at church. I decided to tell the congregation about my new twelve-to-two prayer experiment, and about the strange suggestion that had come out of it.

Wednesday night turned out to be a cold, snowy midwinter evening. Not many people showed up; the farmers, I think, were afraid of being caught in town by a blizzard. Even the couple dozen townspeople who did get out straggled in late and tended to take seats in the rear, which is always a bad sign to a preacher; it means he has a 'cold' congregation to speak to.

I didn't even try to preach a sermon that night. When I stood I asked everyone to come down close 'because I have something I want to show you,' I said. I opened *Life* and held it down for them to see.

'Take a good look at the faces of these boys,' I said. And then I told them how I had burst into tears and how I had got the clear instruction to go to New York, myself, and try to help those boys. My parishioners looked at me stonily. I was not getting through to them at all, and I could understand why. Anyone's natural instinct would be aversion to those boys, not sympathy. I could not understand my own reaction.

Then an amazing thing happened. I told the congregation that I wanted to go to New York, but I had no money. In spite of the fact that there were so few people present, and in spite of the fact that they did not understand what I was trying to do, my parishioners silently came forward that evening and one by one placed an offering on the Communion table. The offering amounted to seventy-five dollars, just about enough to get to New York City and back by car.

Thursday I was ready to go. I had telephoned Gwen and explained to her – rather unsuccessfully, I'm afraid – what I was trying to do.

'You really feel this is the Holy Spirit leading you?' Gwen asked.

'Yes, I do, honey.'

'Well, be sure to take some good warm socks.'

Early Thursday morning I climbed into my old car with Miles Hoover, the Youth Director from the church, and backed out of the driveway. No one saw us off, another indication of the total lack of enthusiasm that accompanied the trip. And this lack wasn't just on the part of others. I felt it myself. I kept asking myself why in the world I was going to New York, carrying a page torn out of *Life*. I kept asking myself why the faces of those boys made me choke up, even now, whenever I looked at them.

'I'm afraid, Miles,' I finally confessed, as we sped along the Pennsylvania Turnpike.

'Afraid?'

'That I may be doing something foolhardy. I just wish there were some way to be sure that this is really God's leading and not some crazy notion of my own.'

We drove along in silence for a while.

'Miles?'

'Uh huh.'

I kept my eyes straight ahead, embarrassed to look at him. 'I want you to try something. Get out your Bible and open it just at random and read me the first passage you put your finger on.'

Miles looked at me as if to accuse me of practicing some kind of superstitious rite, but he did what I asked. He reached into the back seat and got his Bible. Out of the corner of my eye I watched him close his eyes, tilt his head backwards, open the book and plunge his finger decisively onto a spot on the page.

Then he read to himself, and I saw him turn and look at me, but not speak.

'Well,' I said.

The passage was in the 126th Psalm, verses five and six.

'They that sow in tears,' Miles read, 'shall reap in joy. He that goeth forth and weepeth, bearing precious seed, shall doubtless come again with rejoicing, bringing his sheaves with him.'

We were greatly encouraged as we drove on toward New York. And it was a good thing, because it was the last encouragement we were to receive for a long, long time.

Chapter Two

We came into the outskirts of New York along Route 46, which connects the New Jersey Turnpike with the George Washington Bridge. Once again logic was raising difficulties. What was I going to do once I got to the other side of the bridge? I didn't know.

We needed gasoline, so we pulled into a station just short of the bridge. While Miles stayed with the car, I took the *Life* article, went into a phone booth, and called the District Attorney named in the article. When I finally reached the proper office, I tried to sound like a dignified pastor on a divine mission. The Prosecutor's Office was not impressed.

'The District Attorney will not put up with any interference in this case. Good day to you, sir.'

And the line went dead.

I stepped out of the phone booth and stood for a moment beside a pyramid of oil cans, trying to recapture my feeling of mission. We were 350 miles from home and it was getting dark. Weariness, discouragement, and a faint fright gripped me. I felt lonesome. Somehow, standing in the neon dusk of the filling station, having experienced the kind of rebuff I must expect, the guidance I had received in the security of my mountain parish study didn't seem so convincing.

'Hey, David.' It was Miles calling. 'We're blocking the exit here.'

We pulled out onto the highway. Instantly we were locked in a gigantic traffic flow; we couldn't have turned around if we had wanted to. I had never seen so many cars, all in a hurry. They pulled around me and honked at me; the air brakes on gigantic trucks hissed at me.

What a sight the bridge was! A river of red lights on the right – the taillights of the cars in front – and the white glare of oncoming traffic and the immense skyline looming out of the night ahead. I realized suddenly how countrified I really was.

'What do we do now?' I asked Miles at the end of the bridge, where a dozen green signs pointed us to highways whose names meant nothing to us.

'When in doubt,' said Miles, 'follow the car ahead.'

The car ahead, it turned out, was going to upper Manhatten. So did we.

'Look!' said Miles, after we had gone through two red lights and nearly run over a police officer who stood sadly shaking his head after us. 'There's a name I know! Broadway!'

The familiar street name was like a face from home in a strange crowd. We followed Broadway past numbered street signs that worked steadily downward from over 200 to under 50, and suddenly we were in Times Square. We thought of quiet evenings in Philipsburg as Miles read out words from the marquees: 'Naked Secrets', 'Loveless Love', 'Teen-age Girl of the Night', 'Shame'. Great white letters at one theatre spelled out 'For Adults Only', while beneath them a man in a red uniform kept a crowd of restless, pushing children in line.

A few blocks later we came to Macy's, then Gimbels. My heart leaped at the sight of them. Here were names I knew, Gwen ordered things from these stores: the warm socks she'd made me promise to wear came, I thought, from Gimbels. It was a point of contact with the old and tried. I wanted to stick close to those stores.

'Let's look for a hotel near here,' I suggested to Miles.

Across the street was the Martinique; we decided on that. Now there was the problem of parking. There was a car lot across from the hotel, but when the man at the gate said, 'Two dollars overnight,' I backed hastily into the street again.

'It's because we're from out of town,' I told Miles as I drove away with what I hoped was indignant speed. 'They think they can get away with anything if you're a stranger.'

Half an hour later we were back at the parking lot again. 'All right, you win,' I said to the man, who didn't smile. A few minutes later we were in our room on the twelfth floor of the Hotel Martinique. I stood at the window for a long time, looking down at the people and cars below. Every now and again a gust of wind blew clouds of trash and newspaper around the corner. A group of teen-agers were huddled around an open fire across the street. There were five of them. They were dancing in the cold, holding out their hands to the blaze and wondering, no doubt, what they were going to do. I fingered the page from *Life*, in my pocket, and thought how a few months earlier seven others, perhaps something like these boys, had wandered in a cloud of anger and boredom into Highbridge Park.

'I'm going to try the District Attorney's office again,' I said to Miles. To my surprise it was still open. I knew I was making a nuisance of myself but I could think of no other way to reach those boys. I called twice more, and then a third time. And at last I annoyed someone into giving me some information.

'Look,' I was told shortly, 'the only person who can give you permission to see those boys is Judge Davidson himself.'

'How do I get to see Judge Davidson?'

A bored reply: 'He'll be at the trial tomorrow morning. One hundred Court Street. Now good-bye, Reverend. Please don't call here again; we can't help you.'

I tried one more call, this time to Judge Davidson. But the operator told me that his line had been disconnected. She was sorry, no, there was no possible way of getting through.

We went to bed, but I, at least, did not sleep. To my unaccustomed ears every sound of the city at night was filled with menace. I divided the long hours about evenly between wondering what I was doing here and fervent prayers of thanks that, whatever it was, it couldn't keep me here long.

The next morning, shortly after seven o'clock, Miles and I got up, dressed, and checked out of the hotel. We did not eat breakfast. Both of us felt instinctively that some sort of crisis was ahead of us, and we felt that this fast would leave us at our mental and physical best.

If we had known New York better, we would have taken the subway downtown to the courthouse. But we didn't know New York, so we got our car out of the lot, asked directions for Court Street, and once again headed down Broadway.

One hundred Court Street is a mammoth, frightening building to which people flock who are angry with each other and want vengeance. It attracts hundreds every day who have legitimate business there, but it also draws curious, gawking spectators who come to share – without danger – in the anger. One man in particular that day was sounding off outside the courtroom where the Michael Farmer trial was to be reconvened later in the morning.

'Chair's too good for them,' he said to the public in general. He turned to the uniformed guard stationed outside the closed door. 'Got to teach them a lesson, young punks. Make an example out of them.'

The guard hooked his thumbs in his belt and turned his back on the man, as if he had long ago learned that this was the only defense against the self-appointed guardians of justice. By the time we arrived – at 8:30 – there were forty people waiting in the line to enter the courtroom. I discovered later that there were forty-two seats available that day in the spectator section. I have often thought that if we'd stopped for breakfast, all that has happened to me since that morning of February 28, 1958, would have taken a different direction.

For an hour and a half we stood in line, not daring to leave, since there were others waiting for a chance to step into our places. Once, when a court official passed down the line, I pointed to a door farther along the corridor.

'Is that Judge Davidson's chambers?' I asked him.

He nodded.

'Could I see him, do you think?'

The man looked at me and laughed. He didn't answer, just gave a grunt that was half scorn, half amusement, and walked away.

At around ten o'clock a guard opened the courtroom doors and we filed into a little vestibule where each one of us was briefly inspected. We held out our arms; I took it they were looking for weapons.

'They've threatened the Judge's life,' said the man in front of me, turning around while he was being searched. 'The Dragon gang. Said they'd get him in court.'

Miles and I took the last two seats. I found myself next to the man who thought that justice should be faster. 'Those boys should be dead already, don't you think?' he said to me even before we were seated, and then turned to ask his other neighbour the same question before I had a chance to answer.

I was surprised at the size of the courtroom. I had expected an impressive room with hundreds of seats, but I guess that idea had come from Hollywood. Actually, half of the room was taken up by court personnel, another fourth by the press, with only a small section in the rear for the public.

My friend on the right gave me a running commentary on court procedure. A large group of men strolled in from the back of the court, and I was informed that these were the court-appointed lawyers.

'Twenty-seven of them,' my friend said. 'Had to be supplied by the State. Nobody else would defend the scum. Besides, they don't have any money. Spanish boys, you know.'

I didn't know, but said nothing.

'They had to plead "not guilty". State law for first-degree murder. They ought to get the chair, all of them.'

Then the boys themselves came in.

I don't know what I'd been expecting. Men, I suppose. After all this was a murder trial, and it had never really registered with me that children could commit murder. But these were children. Seven stooped, scared, pale, skinny children on trial for their lives for a merciless killing. Each was handcuffed to a guard and each guard, it seemed to me, was unusually husky, as if he had been chosen deliberately for contrast.

The seven boys were escorted to the left of the room, then seated and the handcuffs taken off.

'That's the way to handle them,' said my neighbor. 'Can't be too careful. God, I hate those boys!'

'God seems to be the only one who doesn't,' I said.

'Wha....?'

Someone was pounding on a piece of wood and calling the court to order as in walked the judge, very briskly, while the entire room stood.

I watched the proceedings in silence, but not my neighbour. He expressed himself so emphatically that several times people turned around to stare at us. A girl was on the stand that morning.

'That's the gang's doll,' I learned from next door. 'A doll is a teen whore.'

The girl was shown a knife and asked if she had recognized it. She admitted that it was the knife from which she had wiped blood on the night of the murder. It took all morning to achieve that simple statement.

———

And then, quite suddenly, the proceedings were over.

It took me by surprise – which may, in part, explain what happened next. I didn't have time to think over what I was going to do.

I saw Judge Davidson stand and announce that the court was adjourned. In my mind's eye I saw him leaving that room, stepping through that door, and disappearing forever. It seemed to me that if I didn't see him now, I never would.

'I'm going up there and talk to him,' I whispered to Miles.

'You're out of your mind!'

'If I don't . . .' The judge was gathering his robes together, preparing to leave. With a quick prayer I grasped my Bible in my right hand, hoping it would identify me as a minister, shoved past Miles into the aisle, and ran to the front of the room.

'Your Honour!' I called.

Judge Davidson whirled around, annoyed and angry at the breach of court etiquette.

'Your Honour, please would you respect me as a minister and let me have an audience with you?'

But by now the guards had reached me. I suppose the fact that the judge's life had been threatened was responsible for some of the roughness that followed. Two of them picked me up by the elbows and hustled me up the aisle, while there was a sudden scurrying and shouting in the press section as photographers raced each other to the exit trying to get pictures.

The guards turned me over to two blue uniforms, out in the vestibule.

'Close those doors,' ordered one officer. 'Don't let anyone out of there.'

Then, turning to me, 'All right, Mister. Where's the gun?'

I assured him that I didn't have a gun. Once again I was searched.

'Who were you with? Who else is in there?'

'Miles Hoover. He's our Youth Director.'

They brought Miles in. He was shaken, more with anger and shame, I think, than with fear.

Some of the press managed to get into the room while the police were questioning us. I showed the police my papers of ordination so they'd know I was a bona fide clergyman. They were arguing among themselves about what charges to book me on. The sergeant said he'd find out Judge Davidson's wishes, and while he was gone the reporters pumped me and Miles with more questions. Where were we from? Why had we done it? Were we with the Dragons? Had we stolen those church letters or forged them?

The sergeant came back saying that Judge Davidson didn't want to prefer charges, and that they would let me go this time if I agreed never to come back.

'Don't worry,' said Miles. 'He won't come back.'

They escorted me brusquely out to the corridor. There a semicircle of newsmen were waiting with their cameras cocked. One man asked me:

'Hey, Rev'rn. What's that book you got there?'

'My Bible.'

'You ashamed of it?'

'Of course not.'

'No? Then why you hiding it? Hold it up where we can see it.'

And I was naïve enough to hold it up. Flash bulbs popped, and suddenly I knew how it would come out in the papers: a Bible-waving country preacher, with his hair standing up on his head, interrupts a murder trial.

One, just one, of the reporters was more objective. He was Gabe Pressman, NBC News. He asked me some questions about why I was interested in boys who had committed such a heinous crime.

'Have you ever looked at those boys' faces?'

'Yes. Sure.'

'And you can still ask that question?'

Gabe Pressman smiled ever so slightly. 'I see what you mean. Well, Reverend, you're different from the curiosity-seekers, anyway.'

I was different all right. Different enough to think I had some special divine errand, when all I was doing was playing the fool. Different enough to bring shame to my church, my town, and my family.

As soon as they let us go, we hurried to the parking lot where our car had earned another two-dollar charge. Miles didn't say a word. The minute we got in the car and closed the door, I bowed my head and cried for twenty minutes.

'Let's go home, Miles. Let's get out of here.'

Going back over the George Washington Bridge, I turned and looked once more at the New York skyline. Suddenly I remembered the passage from Psalms that had given us so much encouragement: 'They that sow in tears shall reap in joy.'

What kind of guidance had that been? I began to doubt there was such a thing as getting pinpointed instructions from God.

How would I face my wife, my parents, my church? I had stood before the congregation and told them that God had moved on my heart, and now I must go home and tell them that I had made a mistake and that I did not know the heart of God at all.

Chapter Three

Miles,' I said, when the bridge was fifty miles behind us, 'do you mind very much if we drive home by way of Scranton?'

Miles knew what I was referring to. My parents lived there. I wanted, frankly, to cry on their shoulders a bit.

By the time we reached Scranton, next morning, the story was in the newspapers. The Michael Farmer trial was well covered by the press, but news items on it had begun to run scarce. The grisly aspects of the murder had been explored and editorially shuddered at until the last ounce of horror had been wrung from them. The psychology, sociology, and penology of the case were long since exhausted. Now, just as the flow of ink was threatening to falter, here appeared a bizarre sidelight to warm an editor's heart, and the papers made the most of it.

We were in the outskirts of Scranton before it occurred to me to wonder how my parents would be affected by all this. I'd been as eager to see them as a little boy with a hurt, but now that I was actually here I dreaded the moment of meeting. After all, the name that I had exposed to ridicule was theirs also.

'Maybe,' said Miles as we turned into their driveway, 'they won't have seen it.'

They had seen it. A newspaper was spread out on the kitchen table, turned to the UP account of the wild-eyed, Bible-waving young preacher who had been thrown out of the Michael Farmer murder trial.

Mother and Dad greeted me politely, almost formally.

'David,' Mother said, 'what a . . . pleasant surprise.'

'Hello, son,' said Dad.

I sat down. Miles had tactfully gone for 'a little stroll', knowing that those first few moments should be private ones.

'I know what you're thinking.' I nodded my head toward the newspaper. 'I'll say it for you. How are we ever going to live this down?'

'Well, son,' my father said, 'it's not so much us. It's the church. And you, of course. You could lose your ordination.'

Realizing his great concern for me, I kept silent.

'What are you going to do when you get back to Philipsburg, David?' Mother asked.

'I haven't thought that far yet.'

Mother went to the icebox and got out a bottle of milk.

'Do you mind if I give you a piece of advice?' she asked, pouring me a glass. (She was always trying to put pounds on me.) Often, when Mother was ready to give me advice, she didn't stop to ask my permission. This time, though, she waited, milk bottle in hand, until I had actually nodded my head for her to go on. It was as if she recognized that this was a battle I'd have to fight out by myself, and that I might not want a mother's advice.

'When you get back home, David, don't be too quick to say you were wrong. "The Lord moves in mysterious ways His wonders to perform." It's just possible this is all part of a plan you can't see from where you're standing. I have always believed in your good judgement.'

All the way back to Philipsburg I mulled over Mother's words. What good could possibly come out of this fiasco?

I took Miles to his house and then drove to the parsonage by a back street. If it's possible to sneak into your own driveway with something as big as a car, then that's what I did. I closed the car door so that it wouldn't slam, and I almost tiptoed into my own living room. There was Gwen.

She came over and put her arms around my neck. 'Poor David,' she said. It was only after a long, silent time just-being-together that she finally asked, 'What went wrong?'

I told her in detail what had happened since I'd seen her last, and then I told her of my mother's thought that perhaps nothing *had* gone wrong.

'You're going to have a hard time convincing this town of that, David. The telephone's been ringing.'

And it kept on ringing for the next three days. One of the town officials called to bawl me out. Fellow ministers didn't hesitate to tell me they thought it was cheap publicity. When I finally dared to walk downtown, heads turned to follow me all along the street. One man who was always trying to bring more business into town pumped my hand and slapped me on the back and said:

'Say, Reverend, you really put old Philipsburg on the map!'

Hardest of all was meeting my own parishioners that Sunday. They were polite – and silent. From the pulpit that morning I looked at the problem as squarely as I could.

'I know that all of you must be asking yourselves questions,' I said, talking to two hundred stony faces. 'First of all, you feel for me, and I appreciate that.

'But then, you must be saying to yourselves, "What kind of egoist do we have for a preacher, a man who thinks that every whim he gets is a mandate from God?" This is a legitimate question. It would surely look as though I had confused my own will for God's. I have been humbled and humiliated. Perhaps it was to teach me a lesson.

'And yet, let's ask ourselves honestly: If it is true that the job of us humans here on earth is to do the will of God, can we not expect that in some way He will make that will known to us?' Stony faces, still. No response. I wasn't making a very good case for the life of guidance.

But the congregation was remarkably kind. Most of the people said they thought I had acted foolishly, but that they knew my heart was in the right place. One good lady said, 'We still want you even if nobody else does.' After that memorable statement, she *did* spend a long time explaining that she hadn't meant it to sound like that.

Then a strange thing happened.

In my nightly prayer sessions, one particular verse of Scripture kept occurring to me. It came into my mind again and again: 'All things work together for good to them that love God and are called according to His purpose.'

It came with great force and a sense almost of reassurance, though to the conscious part of my mind nothing reassuring was conveyed. But along with it came an idea so preposterous that for several nights I dismissed it as soon as it appeared.

Go back to New York.

When I had tried ignoring it three nights in a row and found it as persistent as ever, I set about to deal with it. This time I was prepared.

New York, in the first place, was clearly not my cup of tea. I just did not like the place, and I was manifestly unsuited for life there. I revealed my ignorance at every turn, and the very name 'New York' was for me now a symbol of embarrassment. It would be wrong from every point of view to leave Gwen and the children again so soon. I was not going to drive eight hours there and eight hours back for the privilege of making a fool of myself again. As for going back to the congregation with a new request for money, it was out of the question. These farmers and mine workers were already giving more than they should. How would I explain it to them, when I myself did not begin to understand this fresh order to return to the scene of my defeat? I had no better chance than before to see those boys. Less – because now I was typed in the eyes of city officials as a lunatic. Wild horses couldn't drag me to my church with such a suggestion.

And yet, so persistent was this new idea, that on Wednesday night, I stood in the pulpit and asked my parishioners for more money to get me back to New York.

The response of my people was truly amazing. One by one, they again got up on their feet, marched down the aisle and placed an offering on the Communion table. This time, there were many more people in the church, perhaps 150. But the interesting thing is that the offering was almost exactly the same. When the dimes and quarters, and the very occasional bills, were all counted, there was just enough to get to New York again. Seventy dollars had been collected.

The next morning Miles and I were on our way by six. We took the same route, stopped at the same gas station, took the bridge into New York. Crossing the bridge, I prayed, 'Lord, I don't have the least idea why You let things happen as they did last week or why I am coming back into this mess. I do not ask to be shown Your purpose, only that You direct my steps.'

Once again we found Broadway and turned south along this only route we knew. We were driving slowly along when suddenly I had the most incredible feeling that I should get out of the car.

'I'm going to find a place to park,' I said to Miles. 'I want to walk around for a while.' We found an empty meter.

'I'll be back in a while, Miles. I don't even know what it is I'm looking for.'

I left Miles sitting in the car and started walking down the street. I hadn't gone half a block before I heard a voice:

'Hey, Davie!'

I didn't turn around at first, thinking some boy was calling a friend. But the summons came again.

'Hey, Davie. Preacher!'

This time I did turn around. A group of six teen-age boys were leaning against the side of a building beneath a sign saying, 'No Loitering. Police Take Notice.' They were dressed

in tapered trousers and zippered jackets. All but one of them
were smoking, and all of them were bored.

A seventh boy had separated himself from the group and
walked after me. I liked his smile as he spoke.

'Aren't you the preacher they kicked out of the Michael
Farmer trial?'

'Yes. How'd you know?'

'Your picture was all over the place. Your face is kind of
easy to remember.'

'Well, thank you.'

'It's no compliment.'

'You know my name, but I don't know yours.'

'I'm Tommy. I'm the President of the Rebels.'

I asked Tommy, President of the Rebels, if those were
his friends leaning against the 'No Loitering' sign, and he offered
to introduce me. They kept their studiously bored expressions
until Tommy revealed that I had had a run-in with the police.
That was magic with these boys. It was my *carte blanche* with
them. Tommy introduced me with great pride.

'Hey fellows,' he said, 'here's the preacher who was kicked
out of the Farmer trial.'

One by one, the boys unglued themselves from the side
of the building and came up to inspect me. Only one boy did not
budge. He flicked open a knife and began to carve an unprintable
word in the metal frame of the 'No Loitering' sign. While the rest
of us talked, two or three girls joined us.

Tommy asked me about the trial, and I told him I was
interested in helping teen-agers, especially those in the gangs.
The boys, all but the carver, listened attentively, and several of
them mentioned that I was 'one of us.'

'What do you mean, I'm one of you?' I asked.

Their logic was simple. The cops didn't like me; the
cops didn't like them. We were in the same boat, and I was one
of them. This was the first time but by no means the last time

that I heard this logic. Suddenly I caught a glimpse of myself being hauled up that courtroom aisle, and it had a different light on it. I felt the little shiver I always experience in the presence of God's perfect planning.

I didn't have time to think more about it just then, because the boy with the knife at last stepped up to me. His words, although they were phrased in the language of a lonesome boy on the streets, cut my heart more surely than his knife would have been able to do.

'Davie,' the boy said. He hiked his shoulders up to settle his jacket more firmly on his back. When he did, I noticed that the other boys moved back a fraction of a step. Very deliberately, this boy closed and then opened his knife again. He held it out and casually ran the blade down the buttons of my coat, flicking then one by one. Until he had finished this little ritual, he did not speak again.

'Davie,' he said at last, looking me in the eye for the first time, 'you're all right. But Davie, if you ever turn on boys in this town . . .' I felt the knife point press my belly lightly.

'What's your name, young man?' His name was Willie, but it was another boy who told me.

'Willie, I don't know why God brought me to this town. But let me tell you one thing. *He* is on your side. That I can promise you.'

Willie's eyes hadn't left mine. But gradually I felt the pressure of the knife point lessen. And then his eyes broke away. He turned aside.

Tommy adroitly turned the subject. 'Davie, if you want to meet the gangs, why don't you start right here? These guys are all Rebels, and I can show you some GGIs too.'

'GGIs?'

'Grand Gangsters, Incorporated.'

I hadn't been in New York half an hour and already I was being introduced to my second street gang. Tommy gave me street directions, but I couldn't follow them. 'Boy, you *are* a rube aren't you! Nancy!' he called one of the girls standing nearby. 'Take the preacher down to the GGIs, will you?'

The GGIs met in a basement on 134th Street. To reach their 'clubroom' Nancy and I walked down a flight of cement stairs, weaving our way past garbage pails that were chained to the building, past thin cats with stiff filthy fur, past a pile of vodka bottles, until finally Nancy stopped and rapped, two-quick, four-slow, on a door.

A girl opened it. I thought at first that she was playing a joke. She was the perfect clichéd stereotype of a tramp. She had no shoes on, she held a can of beer, a cigarette hung sideways from her lips, her hair was unkempt and the shoulder of her dress was pulled down in a deliberately revealing way. Two things kept me from laughing. This girl's face showed no signs of amusement. And she was a child, a little girl in her teens.

'Maria?' said Nancy. 'Can we come in? I want you to meet a friend.'

Maria shrugged one shoulder – the one holding her dress up – and opened the door wider. The room inside was dark and it took me a while to realize that it was filled with couples. Boys and girls of high school age sat together in this cold and ill-smelling room and I realized with a jolt – Tommy was right: I was a rube – that Maria had probably not taken off her own shoes, nor pulled down her own dress. Someone switched on a wan overhead light bulb. The kids slowly untangled themselves and looked up with the same bored eyes I'd seen in the faces of the Rebels.

'This is that preacher that was kicked out of the Farmer trial,' said Nancy.

Immediately, I had their attention. More important, I had their sympathy. That afternoon I had a chance to preach my first sermon to a New York gang. I didn't try to get a complicated message over to them, just that they were loved. They were loved as they were, there, amid the vodka bottles and the weary, searching sex. God understood what they were looking for when they drank and played with sex, and He yearned for them to have what they were looking for: stimulation and exhilaration and a sense of being sought after. But not out of a cheap bottle in a cold tenement basement. God had so much higher hopes for them.

Once, when I paused, a boy said, 'Keep it up, Preach. You're coming through.'

It was the first time I heard the expression. It meant that I was reaching their hearts, and it was the highest compliment they could have paid my preaching.

I would have left that basement hideout, half an hour later, with a feeling of great encouragement, except for one thing. There, among the GGIs, I had my first encounter with narcotics. Maria – she turned out to be President of the GGI Debs, the girl-gang attached to the GGIs – interrupted me when I said that God could help them toward a new life.

'Not me, Davie. Not me.'

Maria had put down her glass, and she had pulled her dress back up over her shoulder.

'Why not you, Maria?'

In answer, she simply pulled up her sleeve and showed me her inner arm at the elbow.

I didn't understand. 'I don't follow you, Maria.'

'Come here.' Maria walked over beneath the light bulb and held out her arm. I could see little wounds on it like festered mosquito bites. Some were old and blue. Some were fresh and livid. I suddenly knew what this teen-age girl was trying to say to me. She was a dope addict.

'I'm a mainliner, Davie. There's no hope for me, not even from God.'

I looked around the room to see if I could catch in the other youngsters' eyes a sense that Maria was being melodramatic. No one was smiling. In that one fleeting glance into the faces of a circle of kids, I *knew* what I was later to find out in police statistics and hospital reports: medicine does not have an answer to drug addiction. Maria had expressed the opinion of the experts: there was virtually no hope for the 'mainline' addict, the one who injects heroin directly into the bloodstream.

Maria was a mainliner.

Chapter Four

When I got back to our car, still parked on Broadway, Miles seemed truly glad to see me.

'I was afraid you'd gotten mixed up in a murder trial of your own, with you as corpse,' he said.

When I told him about the two gangs I had met within an hour of setting foot in New York, Miles had the same fantastic thought that had come to me.

'You realize, of course, that you'd never have had a chance with them if you hadn't been thrown out of court and got your picture taken?'

We drove downtown, and this time we went in person to the D.A.'s office, not because we were under any illusions about our reception there, but because the only route to those seven boys in prison lay through that office.

'I wish there were some way,' I said, 'to convince you that I have no other motive than those boys' welfare in asking to see them.'

'Reverend, if every word you're saying came straight from that Bible of yours, we still couldn't let you see them. The only way you can see those boys without Judge Davidson's permission is to get a signed permission from each of the parents.'

Here was another avenue opened up!

'Could you give me their names and addresses?'

'I'm sorry. That we would not be at liberty to do.'

Back on the street I pulled the now tattered page from *Life* out of my pocket. Here was the name of the leader of the gang: Luis Alvarez. While Miles stayed with the car, I went into a candy store and changed a five-dollar bill – it was almost our last money – into dimes. Then I started to call all the Alvarezes in the telephone book. There were over two hundred of them in Manhattan alone.

'Is this the residence of Luis Alvarez, the one who is in the Michael Farmer trial?' I would ask.

An offended silence. Angry words. A receiver slammed in my ear. I had used up forty of the dimes, and it was clear that we would never reach our boys this way.

I went outside and joined Miles in the car. We were both discouraged. We didn't have the faintest idea of what to do next. There in the car, with the skyscrapers of lower Manhattan towering over us, I bowed my head. 'Lord,' I prayed, 'if we are here on Your errand, You must guide us. We have reached the limit of our own humble ideas. Lead where we must go, for we do not know.'

We started to drive aimlessly in the direction the car was headed, which happened to be north. We got caught in a mammoth traffic jam at Times Square. When, finally, we extricated ourselves from this, it was only to get lost in Central Park. We drove round and round before we realized that the roads there form a circle. We took an exit – any exit, just to be out of the park. We found ourselves on an avenue that led to the heart of Spanish Harlem. And, suddenly, I had that same incomprehensible urge to get out of the car.

'Let's look for a parking place,' I said to Miles.

We pulled into the first empty space we found. I got out of the car and took a few steps up the street. I stopped, confused. The inner urging had gone away. A group of boys were sitting on a stoop.

'Where does Luis Alvarez live?' I asked one of them.

The boys stared at me sullenly and did not answer. I walked on a way, aimlessly. A young Negro boy came running up the sidewalk after me.

'You looking for Luis Alvarez?'

'Yes.'

He looked at me strangely. 'Him that's in jail for the crippled kid?'

'Yes. Do you know him?'

Still the boy stared at me. 'Is that your car?' he said.

I was getting tired of questions. 'That's my car. Why?'

The boy shrugged. 'Man,' he said, 'you parked right in front of his house.'

I felt bumps form on my flesh. I pointed at the old tenement house in front of which I had parked. 'He lives there?' I asked, almost in a whisper.

The boy nodded. I have questioned God sometimes when prayers have gone unanswered. But answered prayer is still harder to believe. We had asked God to guide us, and He had set us down on Luis Alvarez' doorstep.

'Thank you, Lord.' I said aloud.

'What did you say?'

'Thank you,' I answered, addressing the boy. 'Thank you very much indeed.'

The name 'Alvarez' was on the mailbox in the dingy vestibule, third floor. I raced up the stairs. The third floor hall was dark and smelled of urine and dust. The deep brown walls were made of tin into which a waffle design had been pressed.

'Mr Alvarez?' I called, finding a door with the name painted in neat block letters.

Someone called out in Spanish from the interior of the apartment, and hoping it was an invitation to come in, I pushed the door open a foot and peered through. There, seated in a red overstuffed chair, was a slender man, dark-skinned, holding a rosary. He looked up from his beads and his face lit up.

'You Davie,' he spoke very slowly. 'You are the preacher. The cops, they throw you out.'

'Yes,' I said. I walked in. Mr Alvarez stood.

'I pray that you come,' he said. 'You will help my boy?'

'I want to, Mr Alvarez. But they won't let me in to see Luis. I have to have written permission from you and from the other parents.'

'I give that.' Señor Alvarez got out a pencil and paper from the kitchen drawer. Slowly he wrote that I had his permission to see Luis Alvarez. Then he folded the paper and handed it to me.

'Do you have the names and addresses of the other boys' parents?'

'No,' said Luis' father, and he turned his head slightly. 'You see, that's the trouble. I don't keep so close touch on my son. God He brought you here, He will bring you to the others.'

So, just a few minutes after we had parked at random on a Harlem street, I had my first signed permission. I stepped out of Mr Alvarez' apartment, wondering if it was possible that God had literally steered my car to this address in answer to this father's prayer. My mind grasped for another explanation. Perhaps I had seen the address in a newspaper somewhere and retained it in my subconscious.

But even while I was brooding over this, on my way down the dark, tin-lined stairs, another event occurred which could not be explained by subconscious memory. Rounding a corner, I nearly collided with a young boy, about seventeen, who was running full tilt up the stairs.

'Excuse me,' I said, without stopping.

The boy looked at me, mumbled something, and started to run on. But as I passed beneath an overhanging light, he stopped and looked at me again.

'Preacher?'

I turned. The boy was peering through the darkness to have a better look.

'Aren't you the guy who was thrown out of Luis' trial?'

'I'm David Wilkerson, yes.'

The boy thrust out his hand. 'Well, I'm Angelo Morales, Rev'run. I'm in Luis' gang. You been up to see the Alvarezes?'

'Yes.' I told Angelo that I needed their permission in order to see Luis. And then, suddenly, I saw the hand of God on our meeting. 'Angelo!' I said. 'I have to get permission from *each* boy's parents. Mr Alvarez didn't know where the other boys live. But you do, don't you . . .?'

Angelo drove all over Spanish Harlem with us, locating the families of the six other defendants in the Michael Farmer trial. As we drove, Angelo told us a little about himself: he would have been with the boys that night they 'messed Michael up', except that he had a toothache. He said the boys had not gone into the park with any particular plan in mind: they had just gone out 'rumbling' (looking for trouble). 'If it hadn't been Farmer, they'd of been jitterbugging.'

Jitterbugging, we discovered, meant gang fighting. We learned a lot from Angelo, and we confirmed much that we suspected. The boys in this particular gang – were they all like this? – were bored, lonely and smolderingly angry. They craved excitement, and they took it where they could find it. They craved companionship, and they took that where they could find it.

Angelo had an amazing way of making things clear. He was a bright, appealing boy and he wanted to help us. Both Miles and I agreed that no matter what happened to the rest of our plans, we would keep in touch with Angelo Morales, and we would show him another way.

Within two hours we had every signature.

We said good-bye to Angelo, after getting his address and promising to keep in touch with him. We drove back downtown. Our hearts were singing. In fact, we did sing as we struggled once again through the traffic snarls of Broadway. We rolled the windows up tight and shouted out the good old gospel songs we had learned in childhood. The undeniable miracles that had taken place within the last hours gave us a fresh assurance that, when we stepped out on Christ's promise to lead, doors would swing open all along the way.

How could we know, as we wove our way downtown singing, that a few minutes later the doors would slam shut again with a thud? Because even those signatures did not get us in to see the seven boys.

The District Attorney was very much surprised at seeing us again so soon, and when we produced the required signatures, he looked like a man who beholds the impossible. He called the jail and said that if the boys would see us, we must be allowed in.

It was at the jail itself that a strange and totally unexpected block was thrown in our way, not by the boys, nor by the city officials, but by a fellow clergyman. The prison chaplain who had the boys in his care apparently considered that it would be 'disturbing' to their spiritual welfare to introduce a new personality. Each of the boys had signed a form saying, 'We will talk with Reverend David Wilkerson.' The chaplain struck out the 'will', and wrote in 'will not'. And no amount of pleading would persuade the city that his decision should be overruled.

Once again, we headed back across the George Washington Bridge – very, very puzzled. Why was it that we had received such dramatic encouragement only to have the road end again at a blank wall?

It was while we were driving along the Pennsylvania Turnpike late that night, about halfway back to our little country town, that suddenly I saw a ray of hope in the darkness around us.

'Hah!' I said aloud, and woke Miles abruptly from a nap.

'Hah, what?'

'That's what I'll do.'

'Well, I'm glad it's settled,' said Miles, curling up and closing his eyes again.

The ray of hope was in the form of a man, a remarkable man: my father's father. The hope was that he would let me pay him a visit, to place my puzzlement before him.

Chapter Five

D o you know what I think you're doing?' asked Gwen. We
were having a cup of tea together in the kitchen before I set
out for my grandfather's farm. 'I think you need to feel you're
part of some great tradition, and not out on a limb all by yourself. I think you want to get in touch with the past again, and
furthermore I think you are right. Reach back as far as you can,
David. That's what you need just now.'

I'd phoned Grandpap to say I wanted to see him.

'You come right on, son,' he said. 'We'll have us a talk.'

My grandfather was seventy-nine years old and as full of
vinegar as ever. Grandfather was known all over the country in
the early days. He was of English-Welsh-Dutch descent, and he
himself was the son and the grandson, and perhaps the great-
grandson, of a preacher. The tradition is lost in the early history
of the Protestant Reformation in Western Europe and the British
Isles. As far as I know, since the days when clergymen first
started to marry in the Christian Church, there has been a
Wilkerson in the ministry, and usually in a fiery ministry, too.

It was a long drive from Philipsburg to the farm outside
Toledo, Ohio, where Grandpap was resting in his retirement. I
spent most of the drive 'getting back in touch with my past,'
as Gwen said. It was a lively set of memories, especially when
Grandfather came into view.

Grandpap was born in Cleveland, Tennessee. By the
time he reached his twenties he was already a preacher. It's a

good thing that he was young, because his life was rigorous. Grandfather was a circuit rider, which meant he had to spend a good part of his ministry in the saddle. He'd ride Nellie from one frame church building to another, and usually he was preacher, choir director and sexton all in one. He'd be the first one at the church: he'd light the fire and sweep out the mouse nests and air the place. Then the congregation would arrive, and he'd lead them in some old-time singing, like 'Amazing Grace' and 'What a Friend We Have in Jesus'. And then he'd preach.

Grandpap's preaching was very unorthodox, and some of his convictions shocked his contemporaries. For instance, when my grandfather was a young preacher, it was considered sinful to wear ribbons and feathers. The elders in some churches carried scissors on cords at their side. If a penitent lady came forward to the altar wearing a ribbon in her hat, the scissors went to work, along with a lecture titled, 'How Will You Get to Heaven with All the Ribbons on Your Clothes?'

But Grandpap changed his mind about this kind of thing. As he grew older, he developed what he called 'The Lamb Chop School' of evangelizing.

'You win over people just like you win over a dog,' he used to say. 'You see a dog passing down the street with an old bone in his mouth. You don't grab the bone from him and tell him it's not good for him. He'll growl at you. It's the only thing he has. But you throw a big fat lamb chop down in front of him, and he's going to drop that bone and pick up the lamb chop, his tail wagging to beat the band. And you've got a friend. Instead of going around grabbing bones from people, or cutting feathers off them, I'm going to throw them some lamb chops. Something with real meat and life in it. I'm going to tell them about New Beginnings.

Grandpap preached at tent meetings as well as churches, and to this day, when I go around the country, I hear tales of the way old Jay Wilkerson used to keep those meetings hopping. One time, for instance, he was preaching in a tent in Jamaica,

Long Island. He had a good crowd because it was the Fourth of July weekend and a lot of people were on holiday.

That afternoon, my grandfather had been visiting a friend in the hardware business. Grandpap's friend showed him some new sparkler material that snapped and sparkled and smoked when you stepped on it. He hoped this would be a big item for the Fourth. Grandpap was intrigued and bought some; he put it in a paper bag, then stuck it in his pocket and forgot all about it.

My grandfather talked about the New Life in Christ, but he also talked about hell, and he was sometimes pretty vivid in his descriptions of what this place was going to be like. Grandpap was talking along these lines that July night when his hand happened to wander to his coat pocket and felt the sparkler stuff. Very quietly he picked up a handful of the powder and let it drop behind him on the platform. Then, with perfect dead-pan expression, pretending he never noticed a thing, he continued to talk about hell, while the smoke billowed up behind him and the platform crackled.

Word got around that when Jay Wilkerson spoke about hell, you could almost smell the smoke and see the sparks.

People at first expected my father to be the same maverick Grandfather was. But my father was quite different. He was a minister more than an evangelist. With Grandpap preaching all around the country, my father grew up missing the security of a settled home, and this was reflected in his career. He had only four churches during his entire ministry, whereas Grandpap was in a new church every night. My father built solid, stable churches where he was beloved and sought out in times of trouble.

'I guess it takes both kinds of preachers to make a church,' my father said to me one day, when we were living in Pittsburgh. 'But I do envy your grandfather's ability to shake the pride out of people. We need it in this church.'

We got it, too, the next time Grandpap passed through. (Grandfather was always 'passing through'.)

Dad's church was in a fashionable suburb of Pittsburgh, among the bankers and lawyers and doctors of the city. It was an unusual setting for a Pentecostal church, because our services are likely to be a bit noisy and undignified. But in this case we'd toned them down out of deference to our surroundings. It took my grandfather to show us we were wrong.

When Grandpap paid us this visit, everyone in church was trying to live like his neighbour, very sedate and fashionable.

'And dead,' said Grandpap. 'Why, a man's religion is supposed to give him life!'

Dad shrugged his shoulders and had to agree. And then he made his mistake. He asked Grandpap to preach for him the following Sunday night.

I was at that service, and I'll never forget the look on Dad's face when the very first thing Grandpap did was to take off his dirty overshoes and place them right smack in the middle of the altar rail!

'Now!' said Grandpap standing up and staring out over the startled congregation. 'What is it that bothers you about dirty overshoes on the altar rail? I've smudged your beautiful little church with some dirt. I've hurt your pride, and I'll bet if I'd asked you the question, you'd have said you didn't have any pride.'

Dad was cringing.

'Go ahead and wriggle,' Grandpap said, turning to him. 'You need this too. Where's all the deacons in this church?'

The deacons raised their hands.

'I want you to go around and open all the windows. We're getting ready to make some noise, and I want those bankers and lawyers sitting on their porches of a Sunday night to hear what it's like to be glad in your religion. You are going to preach a sermon tonight – to your neighbours.'

The Grandpap said he wanted everybody in the house to stand. We all stood. He said he wanted us to start marching around the church clapping our hands. And we marched and we clapped. He had us clap for fifteen minutes, and then when we tried to quit he shook his head and we clapped some more. And then he started us singing. Now we were marching and clapping and singing, and every time we slowed down a little Grandpap went and shoved open the windows another inch. I looked at Dad and I knew he was thinking:

'We'll never live it down, but it's a good thing that it's all happening.' Then he started singing louder than anyone.

That was quite a service.

The next day Dad got the first reactions from the neighbours. He went down to the bank on business and, sure enough, sitting behind a big desk with no papers on it, was one of our neighbours. Dad tried to turn away, but the banker called him:

'Say, Reverend Wilkerson.' The banker invited him behind the swinging rail and said, 'That was some singing at your church last night. Everyone's talking about it. We heard that you people could sing, and all this while we've been waiting to hear you. It's the best thing that ever happened in this neighbourhood.'

For the next three years there was a real spirit of freedom and power in that church, and with it I learned a tremendous lesson. 'You've got to preach Pentecost,' said my grandfather when he was talking to Dad later about the service-of-the-muddy-boot. 'When you strip it of everything else, Pentecost stands for power and life. That's what came into the church when the Holy Spirit came down on the day of Pentecost.

'And,' continued Grandpap, pounding the back of his fist into his palm, 'when you have power and life you're going to be robust, and when you're robust you're probably going to make some noise, which is good for you, and you're certainly going to get your boots dirty.'

To Grandpap, getting your boots dirty meant not only getting the soles messed up from walking out where the mud and the need is, it also meant getting the uppers scuffed from kneeling.

Grandpap was a man of prayer, and in this his whole family was like him. He raised my father to be a praying man, and Dad in turn passed this on to me.

'David,' my grandfather asked me once, when he was passing through, 'do you dare to pray for help when you're in trouble?'

It seemed a peculiar question at first, but when Grandpap pressed me on it, I discovered that he was driving at something important. I thanked God often for the good things that came my way, certainly, like parents and home, or food and schooling. And I prayed, generally and evasively, that the Lord would some day in some way choose to work through me. But to pray for specific help, that I rarely did.

'David,' said Grandfather, looking at me – for once – without the suggestion of a twinkle in his eye, 'the day you learn to be publicly specific in your prayers, *that* is the day you will discover power.'

I didn't quite understand what he meant, partly because I was just twelve years old, and partly because I was instinctively afraid of the idea. To be publicly specific, he had said. That meant saying, in the hearing of others, 'I ask for such and such.' It meant taking the risk that the prayer would not be answered.

It was by accident that I was forced, one dreadful day, to discover what Grandpap meant. During all of my childhood, my father had been a very sick man. He had duodenal ulcers, and for more than ten years he was not free of pain.

One day, walking home from school, I saw an ambulance tear past, and when I was still more than a block away from home, I knew where it had been heading. From that distance I could hear my father's screams.

A group of elders from the church sat solemnly in the living room. The doctor wouldn't let me in the room where Dad was, so Mother joined me in the hall.

'Is he going to die, Mom?'

Mother looked me in the eye and decided to tell me the truth. 'The doctor thinks he may live two more hours.'

Just then Dad gave a particularly loud cry of pain and Mother squeezed my shoulder and ran quickly back into the room. 'Here I am, Kenneth,' she said, shutting the door behind her. Before the door closed, however, I saw why the doctor wouldn't allow me in Dad's room. The bedclothes and floor were drenched with blood.

At that moment I remembered Grandfather's promise, 'The day you learn to be publicly specific in your prayers is the day you will discover power.' For a moment I thought of walking in to where the men sat in the living room and announcing that I was praying for my father to get up from his bed a healed man. I couldn't do it. Even in that extremity I could not put my faith out where it might get knocked down.

Ignoring my grandfather's words, I ran just as far away from everyone as I could. I ran down the basement stairs, shut myself up in the coal bin, and there I prayed, trying to substitute volume of voice for the belief that I lacked.

What I didn't realize was that I was praying into a kind of loud-speaker system.

Our house was heated by hot air, and the great trumpet-like pipes branched out from the furnace, beside the coal bin, into every room of the house. My voice was carried up those pipes so that the men from the church, sitting in the living room, suddenly heard a fervent voice pouring out of the walls. The doctor upstairs heard it. My father, lying on his deathbed, heard it.

'Bring David here,' he whispered.

So I was brought upstairs past the staring eyes of the elders and into my father's room. Dad asked Dr Brown to wait in the hall for a moment, then he told Mother to read aloud the twenty-second verse of the twenty-first chapter of Matthew. Mother opened the Bible and turned the pages until she came to the right passage.

'And all things whatsoever ye shall ask in prayer,' she read, 'believing, ye shall receive.'

I felt a tremendous excitement. 'Mother, can't we take that for Dad now?'

So while my father lay limp on his bed, Mother began to read the same passage over and over again. She read it a dozen or so times, and while she was reading I got up from my chair and walked over to Dad's bed and laid my hands on his forehead.

'Jesus,' I prayed, 'Jesus, I believe what You said. Make Daddy well!'

There was one more step. I walked to the door and opened it and said, loud and clear:

'Please come, Dr Brown. I have . . .' (it was hard) 'I have prayed believing that Daddy will get better.'

Dr Brown looked down at my twelve-year-old earnestness and smiled a warm and compassionate and totally unbelieving smile. But that smile turned first to puzzlement and then to astonishment as he bent to examine my father.

'Something has happened,' he said. His voice was so low I could hardly hear. Dr Brown picked up his instruments with fingers that trembled, and tested Dad's blood pressure. 'Kenneth,' he said, raising Dad's eyelids and then feeling his abdomen and then reading his blood pressure again. 'Kenneth, how do you feel?'

'Like strength is flowing into me.'

'Kenneth,' said the doctor, 'I have just witnessed a miracle.'

———

My father was able to get up from his bed in that miraculous moment, and in that same moment I was delivered of any doubts about the power of getting out on a limb in prayer. Driving down to Grandfather's farm that day, so many years later, this was one of the memories I brought with me.

Grandfather, I was glad to see, was as alert as ever. He was a little slower in his movements, but as quick of mind and as full of penetrating wisdom. He sat in an old straight chair, straddling it backwards, and listened intently as I told him about my strange experiences. He let me talk for an hour, interrupting only to ask questions. I finished my narrative with a question of my own.

'What do you make of it, Grandpap? Do you think I had a real call to help the boys in the murder trial?'

'No, I don't,' said Grandfather.

'But so many things . . .' I began.

'I think,' he went on, 'that that door's slammed just about as tight as you'll ever find a door shut, David. I don't think the Lord's going to let you see those seven boys for a long, long time. And I'll tell you why. Because if you see them now, you may figure you've done your duty among the teen-age boys in New York. And I think there are *bigger* plans for you.'

'How do you mean?'

'I've got a feeling, David, son, that you were never intended to see just seven boys, but thousands of boys just like them.'

Grandpap let that sink in. Then he went on.

'I mean all the mixed-up and frightened and lonely boys of New York who might end up murdering for kicks unless you can help them. I have a feeling, David, that the only thing you need do is expand your horizons.'

Grandfather had a way of putting things that left me inspired. From wanting to get away from the city as fast as possible, I suddenly found myself wanting to rush right back and get to work. I said something like this to Grandpap, and he just smiled.

'It's easy to say that, sitting here in this warm kitchen talking to your old grandfather. But wait until you meet more of these boys before you start having visions. They'll be full of hate and sin, worse than you've even heard of. They're just boys, but they know what murder is, and rape, and sodomy. How are you going to handle such things when you meet them?'

I couldn't honestly answer him.

'Let me tell you the answer to my own question, Davie. Instead of looking at these things, you've got to keep your eye focused on the central heart of the Gospel. What would you say that is?'

I looked him in the eye. 'I've heard my own grandfather often enough on this subject,' I said, 'to give him an answer from his own sermons. The heart of the Gospel is change. It is transformation. It is being born again to a new life.'

'You rattle that off pretty smooth, David. Wait until you watch the Lord do it. Then you'll get even more excitement in your voice. But that's the theory. The heart of Christ's message is extremely simple: an encounter with God – a real one – means change.'

I could tell from the way my grandfather was getting restless that our interview was about to end. Grandpap unfolded himself stiffly from his chair and started walking toward the door. Knowing him for a dramatist at heart, I felt that the most important part of our discussion was only now to come out.

'Davie,' said Grandpap with his hand on the farmhouse door, 'I'm still worried about you when you meet the raw life of the city. You've been sheltered. When you meet wickedness in the flesh it could petrify you.

'You know ...' and then Grandpap started off on a story that didn't seem to me to have any relation to his point. 'Some time ago I was taking a walk through the hills when I came across an enormous snake. He was a big one, Davie, three inches thick and four feet long, and he just lay there in the sun looking scary. I was afraid of this thing and I didn't move for a long time, and lo and behold, while I was watching, I saw a miracle. I saw a new birth. I saw that old snake shed its skin and leave it lying there in the sun and go off a new and really beautiful creature.

'When you start your new work in the city, boy, don't you be like I was, petrified by the outward appearance of your boys. God isn't. He's just waiting for each one of them to crawl right out of that old sin-shell and leave it behind. He's waiting and yearning for the new man to come out.

     'Never forget that, David, when you see your snakes, as surely you will, on the sidewalks of New York.'

Chapter Six

When I drove to New York next, it was in a different frame of mind. I was no longer a man with the simple mission of helping seven boys involved in a murder trial. 'But if I'm supposed to be doing something else, too,' I said to myself, 'I wish I could get a clear picture of the task.'

There was a vision that lay just outside my grasp, like a half-remembered dream. I only knew that it had to do with some specific help which I was supposed to give boys like Luis and his friends.

In the meanwhile I did not want to pass up a single opportunity to get in touch with Luis' gang. Sentence had been passed. Four of the boys were to be sent to prison, including Luis himself; three were to be released. Of these three boys, one was to be sent to a special home for psychiatric care; one, I learned, was to be rushed out of the city by his parents; and the last was returning home. I decided to try to get in touch with him.

When I arrived at the address on 125th Street, a new name was in the card holder on the door. I knocked anyhow, and was not really surprised when the boy's mother answered the door. She remembered me from the time I had been there before, and seemed glad to see me.

'Come in,' she said. 'You see how we have changed our name. All the time we were getting angry people at the door. Once they write on the wall: "Get your boy out of town or get him killed."'

In the living room of their four-room apartment, newspapers were stacked several feet high on a chair, on the couch, on the coffee table. They all contained stories of the trial. 'You have no idea, Reverend Wilkerson, what it is like to open your paper each day and see the pictures of your boy, how he is on trial for a murder. Neighbours brought most of these papers here, and then they stayed to complain. To my husband they gave other papers, too, at his work.'

We went into the kitchen which smelled wonderfully of Spanish fried food, and there we talked about plans for the future. 'Are you going to stay here?' I asked.

'We would like to go, but it is hard to leave because of my husband's job.'

'But your son is in danger here.'

'Yes.'

'Would you like to send him to live with my family for a while in Pennsylvania? He would be welcome.'

'No,' said this poor woman, turning her food. 'No, when my boy comes home from that jail we will probably send him away from here, but it will be with his own people. No one will see him. He will be like one who has never lived . . .'

When I left her half an hour later, I turned to say goodbye at the door and saw the writing she had mentioned, scrawled in yellow chalk on the wall. Someone had tried to rub it out, but you could still read, '. . . or get him killed.'

So once again I was prevented from making contact with the boys in Luis' gang. Perhaps I should just assume that there was a purpose in these closed doors. Perhaps it lay in the emerging dream which was haunting me. Unlikely as it seemed, unprepared and even unwilling as I was, I was beginning to face the possibility that somewhere along these streets I would inevitably find what the Quakers call my 'bundle' of responsibility.

'Lord,' I said again as I left the 125th Street area and headed back toward my car, 'if You have work for me in this place, teach me what it is.'

This was the beginning of a four-month-long walk through the streets of New York. During the months of March, April, May, and June of 1958, I drove to the city once every week, using my day off for the trip. I would rise early and make the eight-hour drive, arriving in New York in the early afternoon. Then, until deep into the night, I roamed the streets of the city, driving home in early morning.

These were not idle explorations. The feeling of being guided by a purpose other than my own never left me, though the nature of it was more mysterious than ever. I knew of no other way to respond than to return to the city again and again, holding myself open, waiting always for the direction to become clear.

I remember so clearly the first night of this four-month walk. Maria, before I left her in her dank basement cell, had told me that one of the roughest, most brutal neighbourhoods in all New York was the Bedford-Stuyvesant section of Brooklyn.

'Preacher,' said Maria, 'if you want to see New York at its worst, you just drive across the Brooklyn Bridge and open your eyes.'

Did I really want to see New York at its worst? I wasn't so sure. Yet, from just such a womb were born the seven defendants in the Farmer trial. If I were ever going to raise my sights, as Grandfather suggested, perhaps I would first have to lower my eyes.

So I drove downtown along Broadway, past Times Square, past the Martinique where Miles and I had stayed, and on down to the Brooklyn Bridge. On the other side, I got directions to the Bedford-Stuyvesant section from a police officer. So it was that I drove for the first time into the heart of an area that is supposed to have more murders per square foot of land than any place on earth. How little I realized, as I timidly steered my car along its streets, that they would some day be as familiar to me as the friendly streets of Philipsburg.

Bedford-Stuyvesant was once the home of responsible middle-class families who lived in trim three-story houses with gardens in the rear. It is now a Negro and Puerto Rican ghetto. It was a blistering cold March night when I pulled into the area. I had to drive around many blocks before I could find a place to park, because the city was slow clearing the streets through here and most of the cars were frozen to the kerb between gray mounds of snow. Walking was a hazardous progress through ankle-deep slush and over slippery piles of refuse. Alone, I wandered up and down the streets, watching and listening, and touching life at a level which I, from the safety of my mountains, simply had not known existed.

A drunk lay on the icy sidewalk. When I stooped to help him, he cursed me. I told a policeman at the corner about the sick man, and the officer shrugged his shoulders and said he'd look into it. But when I turned to look back, a block away, the policeman was still standing idly on the corner, swinging his night stick.

Two girls, silhouetted against an open door behind them, chirped to me, 'Hey there, big boy. You looking for company?'

Across the street a group of teen-agers were hanging around a candy store. They wore leather jackets with a curious insignia stencilled on the back. I wanted to talk to them, but I hesitated. Would they listen to me? Would they laugh at me, push me around?

In the end I didn't cross the street – not that night. I just walked some more, past bars and overflowing garbage cans, past storefront churches and police stations and on into an immense housing project with broken windows and broken lights and a broken 'Keep Off the Grass' sign buried in the sooty snow.

On the way back to my car I heard what sounded to me like three quick shots. Then I thought that I must have been mistaken, because no one on the busy street seemed excited, or even interested. Within minutes a police car roared by, siren screaming, to pull nose-forward into the kerb with its light flashing red. Only six people stopped to watch as they brought a man out of a rooming house with his arm hanging limply at his side, dripping blood. It took more than a shot in the shoulder to draw a crowd in Bedford-Stuyvesant.

I went back to my car, and after hanging an old shirt in the window as a symbol of privacy, I lay down, pulled a car rug over me and finally went to sleep.

I wouldn't do that today. I know better. It isn't so much the danger of adult thugs, or even teen-agers. It's the Little People. These are the eight-, nine-, and ten-year-olds who travel on the periphery of the teen-age gangs. These little ones are truly dangerous, because they cultivate violence for its own sake. They have the knives and the guns of their older heroes, and they think they achieve manliness by using them. It's the Little People I'd be afraid of today if I had to sleep in a car on the streets.

But in the morning I woke up safe. Was it my very innocence that kept me? Or was it the words from the 91st Psalm that I said over and over again as I fell asleep:

> *Because you have made the Lord your refuge,*
> *And the Most High your habitation,*
> *No disaster will befall you, nor calamity come*
> *near your tent.*
>
> *For he will give his angels charge over you*
> *To guard you in all your ways.*
> *They will bear you up upon their hands,*
> *Lest you strike your foot upon a stone.*
> *Upon the lion and the adder you may tread;*
>
> *Upon the young lion and the dragon you may*
> *trample.*

———

Bit by bit, during this four-month walk, I got to know the streets. Maria and Angelo were very helpful in this. (I had kept in close touch with Angelo after our first encounter on the stairs of Luis Alvarez' apartment house.)

'Angelo,' I said to him one day as we were walking down a Harlem street together, 'what would you say was the greatest problem boys have in this city?'

'Lonesomeness,' said Angelo quickly.

It was a strange answer; lonesomeness in a city of eight million people. But Angelo said the feeling came because nobody loved you, and that all of his friends in the gangs were basically very lonely boys. The more I came to know New York the more I grew certain that Angelo was right.

Before I became personally involved with the problems of these boys, I had no real idea what a teen-age street gang was. We had gangs of a sort when I was growing up in Pittsburgh. The kids used to get together after school to build a clubhouse in the vacant lot. What went on inside these clubhouses varied somewhat, depending on the age and personality of the kids; but the activity never ranged far from simple talk; talk about girls, talk about automobiles, talk about sports, talk about parents. I suppose it is basic to childhood to want to gang together to explore the adult world out of adult earshot.

There are gangs like this in New York too, simple social congregations that never move beyond that function. But there's another kind of teen-age gang in New York that is something else again. This is the fighting gang, the 'bopping' or 'jitterbugging' gang. These boys are never far from violence. I know of one instance when a fight took two months to plan; but I know of another case when at two o'clock in the afternoon ten boys were standing around a street corner drinking pop, and at four o'clock that same afternoon one of the boys was dead, two others in the hospital: a major war between rival gangs had flared up, raged, and ended in the interval.

There are also, I discovered, various kinds of specialty gangs in the city. In addition to the social gangs and the fighting gangs, there are homosexual gangs. Lesbian gangs and sadist gangs. As I got to know more boys personally, I learned about the wild parties these kids throw in empty apartments after school. Some, for instance, are parties where a group of kids gather together to pull the legs off a cat. Some are pure sex parties. Often, the boys told me, they would gather in a dark corner of a park and circle around a couple, practicing mutual masturbation while the couple went through the sexual act on the ground.

Feeding this side of teen-age gang life is a flood of pornography; many of the boys showed me samples extracted from hidden pockets in their wallets. This is not the Girlie Picture that is sold on the street corner. These are drawings and photographs of unnatural acts between boys and girls, of acts with animals. The children told me that they sometimes spend their afternoons in a basement clubhouse, using these pictures as guides.

————

Grim as fighting and promiscuity and unnaturalness are to encounter among teen-agers, there is one depravity which surpasses them all: dope addiction.

I quickly reached the point where I myself could spot peddlers of marijuana around the schoolyards. They were bold and pushy. They talked with freedom about their trade and told me I ought to try smoking pot myself if I was interested in knowing what it was all about. When I showed one man a newspaper picture of a boy doubled up in pain on a hospital bed, in the throes of withdrawal, he laughed at me.

'Don't worry,' he said, 'that guy was on heroin. A little marijuana won't hurt you at all. It ain't much different than a cigarette. Have one?'

It won't hurt you? Marijuana isn't addictive by itself, but it quickly leads to the use of heroin, which is one of the most cruelly addictive drugs known to man. Once, during my long walk, there was a 'panic', as the user says: a time when drugs were in scarce supply because of a major arrest of smugglers. I was exploring through the Bedford-Stuyvesant section during this time. As I walked down one street I heard a high, piercing scream. No one paid the slightest attention. The screaming went on and on and on ...

'That sounds like someone in pain,' I said to a woman who was resting her arms on a first-floor window sill in the same building.

She lifted her head, listened a minute, and shrugged her shoulders.

'Third floor,' she said. 'It's terrible. He's twenty years old. It's heroin. He's really hooked and can't get a fix.'

'You know who it is?'

'Since he was in diapers.'

'Can't we do something to help him?'

'What, for instance? Death is what would help him now.'

'Can't we take him to a hospital?'

The woman just looked at me. 'Mister,' she said after a while, 'you're new around here, aren't you?'

'Yes.'

'You try to get a hooked boy into one of those hospitals and see where you get.'

How those words would come back to me in the months to come! There is only one public facility in all of New York, Riverside Hospital, where an addicted boy can get help. Facilities there are so overtaxed that admission is slow or impossible. If a boy can't get in at Riverside, he can make application to the only other public hospital in the entire United States where a New York City addict can be admitted: a forbidding-looking federal institution in Lexington, Kentucky, which specializes in the problem.

———————

Fighting, sex, drug addiction: these were dramatic manifestations of the needs of New York's teen-age gang members. But as Angelo said, they were just the outward symbols of a

deep inner need: loneliness. A hunger for some kind of significance in life. The saddest thing I found on this long walk was
how pathetically low these boys' sights were. I listened to some
of them describe their hopes.

Hopes? Can you really call it a hope when a boy's goal
in life is to get a new hat? One with a narrow brim. A hat is a
symbol to these boys. More than once I've seen a youngster shiv-
ering in the street because he doesn't own a coat. But on his head
will be a twenty-five dollar Alpine hat with a jaunty feather.

Or perhaps they'd like to go on a trip. Across the Brooklyn
Bridge into Manhattan, for instance. That would be an adventure!
Some day. Somehow. These boys were pitifully isolated, each in
his own small turf. I met dozens of Brooklyn youngsters who had
never been across the Brooklyn Bridge for fear of the enemy gangs
in Manhattan and the Bronx.

Gradually, from all the visits, a pattern emerged. It was a
pattern of need, starting with loneliness and extending through
the gang wars, the sex parties, the dope addiction, and ending in
an early and ignominious grave. To check my own impressions,
I visited police stations, talked with social workers and parole
officers, and spent many hours in the public library. In the end,
my total impression of the problems of New York teen-agers was
so staggering that I almost quit. And it was at this moment that
the Holy Spirit stepped in to help.

This time, He did not come to my aid in any dramatic
way; He simply gave me an idea. He clarified the vision that had
been so like a dimly recalled dream.

I was driving back to Philipsburg, watching the odo-
meter turn around and around keeping pace with the turnpike
milemarkers as they crept past. Suddenly I was asking myself:
'Suppose you were to be granted a wish for these kids. What
would be the one best thing you could hope for?'

And I knew my answer: that they could begin life all
over again, with the fresh and innocent personalities of newborn
children. And more: that this time as they were growing up they
could be surrounded by love instead of by hate and fear.

But of course this was impossible. How could people already in their teens erase all that had gone before? And how could a new environment be made for them? 'Is this a dream You have put into my heart, Lord? Or am I just weaving a fantasy for myself?'

They've got to start over again, and they've got to be surrounded by love.

The idea came to mind as a complete thought, as clearly as the first order to go to New York. And along with it came into my mind the picture of a house where these new kids could come. A really nice house, all their own, where they would be welcomed – welcomed and loved. They could live in their house any time they wanted to. The door would always be open; there would always be lots and lots of beds, and clothes to wear, and a great big kitchen.

'Oh, Lord,' I said aloud, 'what a wonderful dream this is! But it would take a miracle. A series of miracles such as I've never seen.'

Chapter Seven

I made my next trip to New York a week later, in a strange state of mind. In part I was elated by my new dream; and in part I was deeply depressed and thoroughly confused. The more I learned about the nature of the enemy in the big town, the more my own lack of qualifications to combat him stood out in sharp relief.

The enemy lurked in the social conditions that make up the slums of New York, ready to grab lonesome and love-starved boys. He held out easy promises of security and freedom, of happiness and of retribution. He called his promises by innocent names: Clubs (not murderous gangs); Pot (not narcotics); Fish-Jumps (not an anger-filled, unsatisfying sex stimulation); and Jitterbugging (not a desperate fight to death). He built his victims personalities that were almost impossible to reach. He threw around these boys a wall of thick, protective hardness; he made them proud of being hard.

Against his strength, I considered my own weakness. I had none of the usual weapons. I had no experience. I had no money. I had no organization backing me. I was afraid of the fight.

And suddenly I found myself remembering another occasion when I'd seen a fight coming and had been afraid. It happened years ago when I was a boy, and we had just moved to Pittsburgh. I didn't win any Most Likely to Succeed awards when I was growing up. I was always pretty frail, and even skinnier than I am now, if such a thing is possible. The very idea of a first fight left me shaking.

Still, the funny thing is that, all through my high school years, I never had to fight because I had a reputation for being extremely tough. That ridiculous situation came about in a peculiar way, and the more I thought about it, the more I wondered if it did not have significance for me now.

There was a boy in school named Chuck, who was a bully. He was the first boy I heard about when we got to Pittsburgh. Before we'd unpacked our trunks I learned that Chuck always beat up the new kids, and that I had better be particularly careful because he was especially tough on preachers' kids.

Chuck had me shaking before I ever saw him. What was I going to do when we finally did meet? I asked God this question and an answer came quickly and clearly: *Not by might, nor by power, but by my Spirit.* I knew it was a Bible quotation, and I looked it up just to check on my recollection of the passage. Zechariah 4:6, it was – and then and there I took it for my motto. When the time came to face Chuck, I decided, I would simply lean on this promise; God would give me a holy boldness that would be equal to any bully.

All too soon I had a chance to test my theory. One spring afternoon I started home from school alone. I was wearing new clothes, I remember, which made it particularly important that I should not get into a fight; new clothes in our family were too carefully budgeted to be ruined in a street brawl.

Suddenly, ahead, I saw a boy walking toward me. I knew in an instant that this would be Chuck. He was strutting down the opposite side of the street. But the instant he saw me he crossed over and bore down on me like a heavy, snorting, angry bull. Chuck was an enormous boy. He must have weighed fifty pounds more than I, and he towered above me so that I had to bend my neck to look him in the eye.

Chuck stopped dead in my path, legs spread and hands on hips.

'You're the preacher's kid.'

It wasn't a question, it was a challenge, and I'll admit that in that moment all my hopes of holy boldness vanished. I was scared to the core of me.

'Not by might, nor by power, but by my Spirit. Not by might, nor by power, but by my Spirit, saith the Lord of hosts.' I kept repeating this sentence over and over to myself while Chuck commenced to give his opinion of me. First he picked on the fact that I looked stupid in my new clothes. Then he worked over the obvious truth that I was a weakling. After that he had a few words to say about preachers' kids in general.

'. . . by my Spirit, saith the Lord.' I still had not spoken, but inside me an amazing event was taking place. I felt fear melting, and in its place came confidence and joy. I looked up at Chuck and smiled.

Chuck was getting madder and madder. His face turned red as he challenged me to fight.

Still I smiled.

Chuck started to circle me with his fists clenched, pumping his arms slowly and taking short feints toward me. In his face, though, was a hint of alarm. He could see that, for some unfathomable reason, this little shrimp was truly not afraid.

I circled, too, never taking my eye off his, and all the while I smiled.

Finally, Chuck hit me. It was a hesitant little blow that didn't hurt, and it happened to catch me on balance so I wasn't thrown. I laughed, low and secretly.

Chuck stopped his circling. He dropped his fists. He backed off and then he turned and took off down the street.

Next day at school, I began to hear how I'd beaten up the biggest bully in town. Chuck had been telling everyone. He said I was the toughest guy he ever fought. Apparently he laid it on thick, because always after that I was treated with respect by the entire school. Perhaps I should have told the kids the truth, but I never did. I had a kind of insurance policy in my reputation. And, hating to fight as I did, I wasn't about ready to turn my policy in.

Now I wondered if there wasn't something important in that memory. Wasn't I facing the same problem, an enemy far bigger and more powerful than I? Perhaps there was a curious paradox in my lack of strength. Perhaps in this very weakness lay a kind of power, because I knew absolutely that I could not depend upon myself. I could fool myself into thinking that money, or high-placed connections, or a degree in sociology would be adequate to this situation, because I didn't have these things. If I were right in dreaming about a new beginning and a new environment for these boys and girls, perhaps God would choose just such a palpably ill-equipped person as I, so that the work from the very start would depend on Him alone. 'Not by might, nor by power, but by my Spirit saith the Lord of hosts.'

I decided to take a first step toward making my dream come true. The very first thing I needed to know was whether I had any right to be glimpsing such visions. Was it really possible for teen-age New York gang members and dope addicts to change in the radical way I was dreaming about? I remembered how Grandfather insisted that at the heart of the Gospel message was a transforming experience. I knew by memory the passage in Scripture that he was referring to. "'Verily, verily, I say unto thee," said Jesus, "Except one be born anew, he cannot see the kingdom of God." Nicodemus saith unto him, "How can a man be born when he is old? can he enter a second time into his mother's womb, and be born?" Jesus answered, "Verily, verily, I say unto thee, Except one be born of water and the Spirit, he cannot enter into the kingdom of God. That which is born of the flesh is flesh; and that which is born of the Spirit is spirit."'[1]

So if these boys were going to change dramatically, the transformation would have to come about in their hearts. I knew *I* could never bring this about: it would have to be the work of the Holy Spirit. But perhaps I could act as a channel through which the Spirit could reach these boys.

---

[1]John 3:3-6

There was one way to find out. So far, I had only walked and listened in the city. Now I would make a move. I would speak to these boys, trusting the Holy Spirit to reach them where I could not. I started making inquiries around New York: what were the toughest, hardest gangs in town? Time and again two names recurred – the Chaplains and the Mau Maus. Both were in Fort Greene, Brooklyn.

These gangs have their turfs in one of the world's largest housing developments: Fort Greene Projects. More than thirty thousand people live in these towering apartments, most of them Negro and Puerto Rican, and a heavy percentage of them on relief.

The fighting gangs that have been spawned in this area are segregated: the Chaplains are Negro boys; the Mau Maus, Spanish. The two gangs do not fight each other, but join together to protect their turf against outside gangs. And now they had declared war on the police.

The boys had a rather original method of attack. They waited on a rooftop with a sandbag balanced on the ledge. When a police officer passed below, they tried to drop the eighty-pound bag on him. Their timing was not yet perfected and so far they had missed. But they were getting closer. The police in retaliation were using their night sticks at the slightest provocation, and prohibiting more than two or three boys to gather together at a time.

I decided there could be no more telling testing-ground for the Holy Spirit than Fort Greene. Early one Friday morning I picked up a friend of mine, a trumpet player named Jimmy Stahl, and the two of us drove over the Brooklyn Bridge and into the teeming brick and glass jungle called Fort Greene Housing Project. We parked our car near the public school on Edward Street, and began our experiment.

'You stand here near this lamp post,' I told Jimmy, 'and start blowing. If we get a crowd, I can step up on the base of the post and talk to them.'

'What do you want me to play?'

'Why not "Onward Christian Soldiers"?'

So Jimmy began to play 'Onward Christian Soldiers' on his trumpet. He played it over and over. He made it lively and he made it loud.

Windows of the walk-ups across the street flew open and heads popped out. Then children began to swarm out of the buildings. Dozens of little children. They were excited by the music and kept asking:

'Is a circus coming, Mister? Are we going to have a parade?'

I told Jimmy just to keep blowing.

Next, the teen-agers began to arrive. They all seemed to be in uniform. Some of the boys wore brilliant red jackets with black armbands and the two letters 'MM' sewn boldly on the back. Others wore tight tapering trousers, bright shirts and continental shoes with thin soles and pointed toes; these boys carried canes. Just about every teen-ager there wore a sharp-looking Alpine hat with a narrow brim; just about every one also wore sunglasses.

'Lord,' I said to myself, 'they're reaching for something fine here. They all want to belong to something bigger than they are. They all want not to be alone.'

After Jimmy played his piece fifteen or twenty times, a crowd of perhaps a hundred boys and girls had gathered. They milled about shouting to each other and to us, obscenities mingled with the catcalls. I climbed up on the lamp base and began to talk. The uproar increased. I didn't know what to do next. Jimmy was shaking his head. 'They can't hear you!' he formed with his lips.

And at that moment the problem was taken out of my hands. There was a sudden lull in the shouts from the kids. Over their heads I saw a police car pull to the kerb. Officers stepped out and started working their way through the crowd, poking fiercely with their night sticks.

'All right. Break it up. Move on.'

The youngsters parted to let the police through but closed ranks again behind them.

'Get down from there,' one of the officers said to me. When I was facing him, he said, 'What are you trying to do, start a riot?'

'I'm preaching.'

'Well, you're not preaching here. We've got enough trouble in this neighbourhood without having a mob scene on our hands.'

Now the boys and girls got into the act. They shouted that the police couldn't stop me from preaching. It was against the Constitution, they said. The police disagreed. Before Jimmy and I knew what was happening, we were being shoved bodily through the crowd toward the police car.

At the station house, I picked up the theme the kids had used. 'Let me ask you something,' I said. 'Isn't it my right as a citizen to speak on a public street?'

'You can,' admitted the police, 'as long as you speak under an American flag.'

So half an hour later Jimmy started to blow 'Onward Christian Soldiers' again. This time we had an enormous American flag floating behind us, borrowed from the sympathetic principal of the school. And this time, instead of preaching from a lamp post base, I had a piano stool.

Jimmy blew to the north and to the south, to the east and to the west. Again windows flew open, and small children swarmed around us. And again we were faced, a few minutes later, with a hooting, catcalling mob. The only difference was that now we were heroes, because once again we had been tapped by the arm of the law.

Our new popularity, though, did not improve the manners of our audience. I stood on my stool and once again tried to raise my voice above the din.

'I am a country preacher,' I told them, 'three hundred miles from home, and I have a message for you.'

Nobody was listening. Directly in front of me a boy and girl were doing the Fish, the grinding hips that brought whistles and clapping from onlookers. Others picked it up, cigarettes hanging sideways from their mouths, bodies quivering with excitement. It was hardly the setting for a sermon.

In despair, I bowed my head.

'Lord,' I said, 'I can't even get their attention. If You are doing a work here, I will have to ask You even for this.'

While I was still praying, the change began.

It was the smallest children who settled down first. But when I opened my eyes I noticed that a lot of the older boys who had been leaning up against the school fence, smoking, had straightened up, taken their hats off and were now standing with heads slightly bowed.

I was so startled by the sudden silence that I was at a loss for words.

When finally I did begin to speak, I chose John 3:16 as my text: 'For God so loved the world that He gave His only begotten Son that whosoever believeth in Him should not perish, but have everlasting life.' I told them that God loved them as they were, right then. He knew what they were. He knew their hatred and their anger. He knew that some of them had committed murder. But God also saw what they were going to be in the future, not only what they had been in the past.

That was all. I had said what I had to say, and I stopped.

A heavy, eloquent silence hung over the street. I could hear the flag flapping in a light breeze. I told the boys and girls then that I was going to ask for something special to happen to them. I was going to ask for a miracle, that in the next moment their lives be completely changed.

I bowed my head again and prayed that the Holy Spirit do His work. I raised my head. Nobody moved. I asked if there was anyone who wanted to come up front where we could talk. No response.

It was an awkward situation. I had made an experiment in letting the Spirit lead, and He didn't seem to be leading anywhere.

And then suddenly I heard myself saying, without any intention on my part:

'All right, now. They tell me that you've got a couple of pretty tough gangs here in Fort Greene. I want to talk to your Presidents and your Vice-Presidents. If you are so big and tough, you won't mind coming up and shaking hands with a skinny preacher.'

I still don't know why I said it, but as I look back on it now, it was perhaps the best thing I could possibly have said. For a minute, nobody stirred. Then from the rear someone called,

'What's the matter, Buckboard? You scared?'

Slowly a big coloured boy left his station at the rear of the crowd and started to work forward. A second boy followed. This one was carrying a cane, and both were wearing sunglasses. On their way through the crowd they picked up two more boys and all four grouped themselves in front of the piano stool.

The big one stepped forward another few inches.

'Slip me some skin, Preacher,' he said. 'I'm Buckboard, President of the Chaplains.'

I was still innocent of the slang of New York, and when he held out his hand I tried to grasp it. 'Just slip it, Preach,' said Buckboard, and he slid his open palm along mine. He stood for a minute, examining me curiously. 'You're all right, Preacher. You really bugged me.'

Buckboard then introduced me to his Vice-President, Stagecoach, and to his two War Lords.

What was I going to do now? With my heart pounding, I nodded to Jimmy, and we walked with the four boys a few yards away from the crowd. Stagecoach kept saying that our message was 'coming through'.

'You know, Davie,' he said, 'there's a little old lady comes around here with a black cape and a basket of candy bars, and she's always after the boys to stop bopping. She's okay but she never comes through.'

I told the four boys it wasn't I who was coming through but the Holy Spirit. I told them He was trying to reach inside their pride . . . 'and your arrogance, too,' I said, looking directly in their eyes, 'and your complacency. That's all just a shell to hide the real, scared, lonely you. The Holy Spirit wants to get inside that shell and help you start all over again.'

'What we supposed to do, man?'

I looked at Jimmy, but his expression didn't help me. In a church I might have asked these boys to come forward and kneel at the altar. But how could you ask anyone to do that on a public street, in front of friends?

Still, maybe it was just such a bold step that was needed. The change in their lives that we were asking was drastic, so maybe the symbol had to be drastic too.

'What are you supposed to do?' I said. 'Why, I want you to kneel down right here on the street and ask the Holy Spirit to come into your lives so that you will become new men. "New creatures in Christ" is what the Bible says: this can happen to you too.'

There was a long pause. For the first time I was vaguely aware of the crowd that was waiting, very quietly, to see what was going to happen. Finally Stagecoach said, in a voice that was strangely hoarse:

'Buckboard? You want to? I will if you will.'

And before my astonished eyes, these two leaders of one of the most feared fighting gangs in all of New York slowly dropped to their knees. Their War Lords followed their lead. They took their hats off and held them respectfully in front of them. Two of the boys had been smoking. Each took his cigarette out of his mouth and flipped it away, where it lay smoldering in the gutter while I said a very short prayer.

'Lord Jesus,' I said, 'here are four of your own children, doing something that is very, very hard. They are kneeling here before everyone and asking You to come into their hearts and make them new. They want You to take away the hate, and the fighting, and the loneliness. They want to *know* for the first time in their lives that they are really loved. They are asking this of You, Lord, and You will not disappoint them. Amen.'

Buckboard and Stagecoach got up. The two War Lords followed. They did not lift their heads. I suggested they might want to get off by themselves for a while, maybe find a church somewhere.

Still without speaking, the boys turned and started to make their way through the crowd. Someone called out,

'Hey, Buckboard! What's it like when you got religion?'

Buckboard told them to lay off and he was taunted no more. I suppose if someone had really rubbed him the wrong way, he wouldn't have been saved enough to take it non-violently.

Jimmy and I left Fort Greene with our heads swimming. The fact was that we had not expected God to answer us in quite such a dramatic manner. Buckboard, Stagecoach, and two War Lords falling to their knees on a street corner: it was just too much to believe.

Frankly, we'd been better prepared for the reaction of the Mau Mau leaders. They were there in the crowd, too, watching the transformation in Buckboard and Stagecoach with mingled contempt and fascination. After the Chaplains had departed, the crowd began to call for them.

'Israel! Nicky! You're next! Come on, them Niggers weren't afraid. You going to chicken out? Such shouts urged them forward.

Israel, the president of the gang, was as nice a boy as I've met: he stuck out his hand and shook mine like a gentleman.

Nicky was something else. I remember thinking, as I looked at him, that's the hardest face I have ever seen.

'How do you do, Nicky,' I said.

He left me standing with my hand outstretched. He wouldn't even look at me. He was puffing away at a cigarette, shooting nervous little jets of smoke out the side of his mouth.

'Go to Hell, Preacher,' he said. He had an odd, strangled way of speaking and he stuttered badly over some of his sounds.

'You don't think much of me, Nicky,' I said, 'but I feel different about you. I love you, Nicky.' I took a step toward him.

'You come near me, Preacher,' he said, in that tortured voice, 'I'll kill you.'

'You could do that,' I agreed. 'You could cut me in a thousand pieces and lay them out in the street and every piece would love you.' But as I said it, I was thinking: and it wouldn't do a bit of good – not with you, Nicky – there's no love on earth that could reach you.

Before we left Brooklyn we put Buckboard and Stagecoach in touch with a local minister who could follow their spiritual growing pains. 'But I think,' I said to Jimmy, 'we'd better check in on them from time to time, too.' To be perfectly honest, neither one of us could rid himself of the suspicion that the boys were having some fun with us.

But when I intimated as much to Gwen, on my return home, she scolded me.

'David Wilkerson,' she said, 'don't you realize that you got exactly what you wanted? You asked the Holy Spirit for a miracle and now that you've got one you're trying to argue it away. People who don't believe in miracles shouldn't pray for them.'

Chapter Eight

It seemed to me that I had passed the first milestone on the road toward my dream. I had been given hope, almost more than I could assimilate. I even dared to hope that perhaps I would be allowed at last to see Luis. I heard from Angelo that Luis was supposed to be transferred to the Elmira, New York, prison.

'Do you think I could get to see him?' I asked.

'Not a chance, Davie. You'd have to go through channels, and once they learned you were the preacher at the trial, they'd never let you in.'

Still, I wanted to try. The next preaching engagement that took me to the vicinity of Elmira, I made inquiries into the procedure for getting to see a boy. I was told to write a letter, stating my relationship with the prisoner and why I wanted to see him. The request would be considered.

So that was that: I'd have to tell the truth and I'd never be allowed in. But I did hear that some boys were being transferred to Elmira that very day. I went down to the station and waited. When the train came in, a group of about twenty boys was marched off. I scanned each of their faces, but Luis was not among them.

'Do you know Luis Alvarez?' I asked, walking up to one of the boys, who managed to say 'no' before the guard testily shut us off.

'Well,' I said to myself on the way back to Philipsburg,

'it looks as if I'm not going to see those boys. Perhaps I never will. Lord, let me have the grace to accept this if it is Your will.'

But if the Holy Spirit was still closing that door to me, He was opening others. One warm night in early spring, 1958, I was walking through a milling, noisy street in Spanish Harlem when I heard the sound of singing.

I was surprised to recognize the tune as a gospel song, although the words were in Spanish. There was no church nearby: the music seemed to come from a window in one of the walk-up tenements I was passing.

'Who is that singing?' I asked a young man who was sitting on the fender of an automobile smoking a cigarette.

The boy cocked his head to listen, as if the music had become such a part of the background noises of the city that he no longer heard it.

'That's some kind of church,' he said, jerking his thumb toward the door. 'Upstairs. Second floor.'

So, I walked up the stairs and knocked on a door. It opened slowly, but when the light hit my face, the woman standing inside gave a little shriek. In her excitement she half closed the door on me, and turned around rattling off something in Spanish. Soon the doorway was filled with smiling, friendly people. They took me by the arm and pulled me into the apartment.

'You are David!' one man said. 'Aren't you David, the preacher who was thrown out of court?'

It turned out that this was what is known as an out-station church, in the Spanish branch of the Assemblies of God. The people of an 'out-station' meet in private homes until they can afford to build. They had followed the Michael Farmer trial closely and had seen my picture.

'We have been praying for you, and now you are here,' one man said. His name was Vincente Ortez and he was the minister of the little church. 'We want to hear how you came to be at the trial,' he said.

So that night, I had a chance to tell a group of people from my own church about the way God seemed to be leading me into New York's streets. I told them what I'd learned about the problems boys and girls faced with the gangs, and with drink and narcotics. I told them, too, about my dream, and about the first milestone I had passed. 'I think it was God who put that idea into my head, "They've got to begin again, and they've got to be surrounded with love,"' I said, summing up. 'We've seen how the Holy Spirit can reach them right on the street. I for one think it's a magnificent beginning. Who knows, maybe some day they'll even have their house!'

It turned out to be an impassioned speech. I found that I was more excited about the problems these young people face then I had guessed. By the time I had finished, I could see that these good people felt my grief and urgency at the need.

When I finally sat down, several of these men and women held a brief discussion. They spoke excitedly for a few minutes, and then pushed Reverend Ortez forward as spokesman.

'Do you think,' he said, 'that you could come back tomorrow to talk to us, when we could have some more ministers in to hear you?' I said that I could.

And as quietly as that, a new ministry was born. Like most things born of the Spirit, it came simply, humbly, without fanfare. Certainly, none of us that night knew what had begun.

'What's your address here?' Reverend Ortez asked. 'Where can we call you about the time and place?'

I had to admit that I had no address. I didn't have the money even for a cheap hotel room. 'I am, in fact,' I said, 'sleeping in my car.'

Real alarm came over Reverend Ortez' face. 'You mustn't do that,' he said, and when he had translated what I'd said, everyone in the room agreed. 'It's dangerous. More dangerous than you know. You must come here, to our house. You must spend this night and any night you are in town right here with us.'

I accepted this kindness gratefully. Reverend Ortez introduced me to his wife, Delia, and I was shown to a simple bare room with a bunk bed in it. But I was made to feel welcome, and I have never slept better than I did that first night off the streets. I learned later that this remarkable couple kept nothing for themselves beyond the bare necessities of existence: everything else was given away to the glory of God.

———

The next morning I spent in prayer. I sensed that it was far more than coincidence that I had dropped into that little home-church. What was going to happen now, I could not imagine, but I wanted to hold myself as flexible as possible, ready to step out in whatever direction the Holy Spirit should point.

While I was at prayer, Reverend Ortez and his wife must have been constantly on the telephone. By the time we arrived at the church where the meeting was to take place, representatives of sixty-five Spanish Assemblies were gathered to hear what I had to say.

And I had no idea, as I climbed into the pulpit, what that should be. What should I tell them? Why was this opportunity being given me to speak to these people? This time I related the events that had brought me to the city, told about the embarrassment of the trial, and of the puzzling, gnawing feeling I'd had ever since that behind these seeming mistakes was a purpose that I had but barely glimpsed.

'I'll tell you frankly that I don't know what I am supposed to do next. The experience at Fort Greene may have been a one-time piece of good luck. I have no idea that it could be repeated on a larger scale.'

Before the meeting was over, those sixty-five churches had come forward with a plan of action which would determine whether or not it had been a one-time experience. They would hold a mass rally for teen-agers in St Nicholas Arena, a prize-fight centre in New York, where I could address many gangs at once.

I was hesitant. In the first place I wasn't sure that mass meetings were the right approach. 'And then there's the very practical matter of money,' I said. 'It would take thousands of dollars to rent a big arena.'

Suddenly there was a commotion in the back of the church.

A man had jumped to his feet, and was shouting something. I finally made it out. 'Davie,' he was saying, 'everything's all right. Everything is going to be all right.'

I thought he was some kind of fanatic and paid no attention. But after the meeting, the man came up and introduced himself. He was Benigno Delgado, an attorney. Once again he repeated his statement that everything was going to be all right.

'Davie, you go to St Nicholas Arena,' he said. 'You rent it, and talk to these kids. Everything will work out.'

I honestly thought he was one of these excitable, if harmless, visionaries of which every church seems to attract a few. But Mr Delgado saw the quizzical look on my face, and pulled from his pocket the largest roll of bills I had ever seen. 'You talk to those children, Davie. I will rent the arena.' And so he did.

This was how, literally overnight, I became involved in a city-wide youth rally, scheduled to be held in St Nicholas Arena during the second week of July, 1958.

When I returned to Philipsburg with the news, everyone became excited.

Only Gwen was a little silent. 'You realize,' she said at last, 'that that's just when the baby's due.'

I hadn't realized. But how can a husband say a thing like that to his wife? I mumbled something or other about the baby coming late. Gwen laughed.

'It'll be right on time,' she said, 'and you'll have your head in the clouds somewhere and won't even know it, and one day I'll present you with a little bundle and you'll look at it in astonishment. I don't think you really know a child exists anyway until he walks up to you and says, "Daddy." '

Which is doubtless true.

The church in Philipsburg was most generous, not only with its money support during the next two months when I could give it so little of my attention, but with its enthusiasm. I'd been keeping everyone posted on my trips to the city, telling of the tremendous problems these twelve-, thirteen-, fourteen-year-old boys and girls were facing. So they knew how much a part they were of anything the Lord was planning for New York.

I took my vacation to coincide with the rally in order to be away from the church as little as possible, but still, as July approached, I found myself spending more and more time in the Ortez apartment. We got splendid help from the Spanish churches. They supplied us with street workers who posted bulletins all over New York announcing the week-long meetings. They trained batteries of counsellors to be available in the dressing rooms of the arena for boys and girls who might decide to try a new beginning. They arranged for music and ushers and they handled the practical arrangements with the arena.

All I had to do was supply the teen-agers.

That had seemed such a simple thing when it was first proposed. But the closer we came to zero hour, the more I doubted the wisdom of this big rally.

Walking the streets, I'd talked to hundreds of boys and girls but I'd never, until now, grasped what it was like to be inside their desperation. The simple prospect of travelling a few miles and entering a large building, so routine to you and me, loomed for them as an immense and peril-filled undertaking. They were afraid in the first place to leave their own turfs: afraid that as they passed through another gang's territory they would be jumped. Then they were afraid of large aggregations of people, afraid of their own hates and prejudices, afraid that their anger and insecurity would erupt out of control into bloody fighting.

Strangest of all, they were afraid that something in the rally might make them cry. Bit by bit I came to realize the horror these young people have of tears.

What is it about tears that should be so terrifying? I asked them again and again, and each time got the impression that tears to them were a sign of softness, of weakness and childishness in a harsh world where only the tough survive.

Yet I knew from my work in the church how important a role tears play in making a man whole. I think I could almost put it down as a rule that the touch of God is marked by tears. When finally we let the Holy Spirit into our innermost sanctuary, the reaction is to cry. I have seen it happen again and again. Deep soul-shaking tears, weeping rather than crying. It comes when that last barrier is down and you surrender yourself to health and to wholeness.

And when it does come, it ushers forth such a new personality that, from the days of Christ on, the experience has been spoken of as a birth. 'You must be born again,' said Jesus. And the paradox is this: at the heart of this newborn personality is joy; yet the joy is ushered in by tears.

What instinct was it that told these boys and girls they might have to cry if they came into contact with God? They had their own way of expressing this fear, of course. I paid return visits to the gangs I had met, the Rebels and the GGIs, the Chaplains and the Mau Maus, inviting them to the rally, and everywhere it was the same. 'You're not going to bug me, preacher. You're not going to get me bawling.'

Everywhere the same fear of the unknown, the same clinging to the familiar no matter how wretched, the same resistance to change.

One night, some time after I had been to the basement hide-out of the GGIs with the news of the rally, there was a knock on the door of the Ortez apartment. Mrs Ortez looked at her husband with raised eyebrows; he shook his head: no, he wasn't expecting anyone. Mrs Ortez put down a knife with which she had been slicing meat and walked to the door.

There stood Maria. As soon as she stepped into the room I knew that she was high on heroin. Her eyes shone with an unnatural brightness; her hair was all over her face; her hands shook at her side.

'Maria!' I said, getting up. 'Come in.'

Maria came into the centre of the room and demanded in a brusque, belligerent manner to know why we were trying to break up her old gang.

'How do you mean, Maria?' said Delia Ortez.

'Coming down and trying to get the kids to a church service. I know you. You want to break us up.'

Maria began to curse us roundly. Vincente Ortez half rose in his chair in protest, then settled back down again in a gesture that said, 'Go ahead, Maria. I'd rather you express it here than out on the street.'

One of the Ortez children came into the room and Delia moved instinctively to stand next to the child. In that moment Maria rushed to the table where Delia had laid the butcher knife. One sweeping movement and the knife was in her fist, its long blade flashing. Delia jumped quickly between Maria and the child. Vincente leapt to his feet and started across the room.

'Stand back!' yelled Maria. Vincente stopped, because the girl had lifted the knife to her own neck. 'Ha!' she said. 'I'm going to cut my throat. I'm going to stick myself like a pig and you're going to watch.'

All of us in that room knew enough about the despair of the narcotic addict to know this was no dramatic and idle pose. Delia started talking rapidly about the long and wonderful life Maria had ahead of her. 'God needs you, Maria,' said Delia over and over again.

Slowly, over a five-minute period, while Delia never stopped talking, Maria's knife slipped lower and lower until finally it hung from her hand down at her hip. Still talking, Delia was inching closer and at last, with one beautiful and agile leap, she knocked the knife from Maria's hand.

It clattered to the floor.

It spun round and round. The child began to cry.

Maria made no effort to get the knife again. She simply stood in the centre of the room, the most forlorn bundle of dejection I had ever encountered. Suddenly she began to moan. She hid her face in her hands. 'There's no out for me,' she said. 'I'm hooked and there's no way out.'

'Why don't you give God a chance with you?' I asked her.

'No. That's not for me.'

'Well, at least let the other kids come. Think; maybe they can find the way out before it's too late.'

Maria straightened up. She seemed to have gotten back her composure. She shrugged her shoulders. 'It depends if you've got a good show,' said Maria. And with that, she turned and walked out of the Ortez apartment, head high and hips swinging.

Chapter Nine

July arrived with amazing speed. A show it was, in many senses, that we were putting on at St Nick's, and I had never appreciated how much simple legwork went into mounting a show. To transport the young people through the enemy territory they were so afraid of, we set up a system of special buses which would pick up each gang on its own turf and take it nonstop to the arena. Workers from the sixty-five sponsoring churches combed the streets, alerting gang members to the arrangements.

I made my last trip home to see Gwen just before the crusade began.

'David,' she said, 'I'm not going to pretend that I didn't wish you were home for the new baby.'

'I know.' It was a subject we didn't mention often. My mother-in-law was provoked at me for going away just when the baby was due. She told me that we men were all the same, and that true Christianity started at home, and that if I didn't have better respect for my wife, I didn't deserve her. Which remarks stung all the more because they contained an element of truth.

'But Dave,' Gwen went on, 'babies have been born before without the father's assistance. The doctor wouldn't let you hold my hand anyhow, and that's what I'd want. So I'd miss you even if you were in the next room. You feel you've got to go, don't you?'

'Yes.'

'Then go gladly. And God be with you, David.'

I left Gwen, standing in the yard waving, very large with child. When I saw her next the miracle of birth would have occurred. I wondered if I would have new births to report to her too.

After the first four days of the meetings, I doubted it.

We had been so busy getting ready that the letdown of the rally itself was all the harder to take. Rally? The very word suggests swarms of enthusiastic people. Nothing could be further from the case.

On the fourth night a hundred people showed up. The arena will hold seven thousand.

I remember standing at a little window on the balcony, where I could watch the teen-agers arrive without being seen myself. Each night I had hoped for a breakthrough. Each night only a handful of people straggled off the special buses and made their way into the arena.

I went backstage. The counsellors and youth workers from the churches were all standing around on one foot and then the other, trying to find encouraging words.

'You know it isn't numbers that count, Davie. It's quality not quantity.' But we all knew we were getting neither quality nor quantity. The teen-agers who did come, came for a show. It was difficult talking to an empty auditorium with the youngsters blowing smoke rings in your face and making lewd remarks.

The worst of it was what the kids call 'breaking up.' Whenever they didn't understand something, or didn't believe it, they began to laugh. I got so I dreaded to go out on the platform for fear of that laughter. The fourth night was the worst I'd ever known it. I did my best to build the meeting to a certain pitch of dignity and solemnity, and then, all of a sudden one of the ringleaders snickered. Someone else picked it up and, before I could stop it, the whole bunch of them were holding their sides with laughter.

I cut the meeting short that night and went home broken-hearted and ready to quit.

'Lord,' I said in real anger, 'we're not even beginning to reach these boys and girls. What am I supposed to do?'

And as always – why is it I have to learn this again every time? – when I really asked, I was really answered.

I met Little Jo-Jo the next day in Brooklyn. Jo-Jo was pointed out to me as the President of the Coney Island Dragons, one of the largest street gangs in the city. The boy who pointed him out wouldn't introduce us. 'Little Jo-Jo might not like it, Dave.' So I walked up to this boy alone and stuck out my hand.

Jo-Jo's first act was to slap me across the palm. Then he leaned over and spat on my shoes. In the gangs this is the highest sign of contempt. He walked away and sat down on a bench with his back to me.

I walked over and sat beside him. I said, 'Jo-Jo, where do you live?'

'Preacher, I don't want to talk to you. I don't want to have anything to do with you.'

'But I want to have something to do with you,' I said. 'I'm going to stay here until I find out where you live.'

'Preacher,' said Jo-Jo, 'you're sitting in my parlour.'

'Well, where do you go when it rains?'

He said, 'I move down to my suite in the subway.'

Jo-Jo had on a pair of old canvas shoes. His toe was sticking out on the right foot and he had a dirty black shirt on and a too-big pair of khaki trousers. He looked down at my shoes. They were brand new and right then I was remembering Grandpap's muddy boots and kicking myself for being a fool.

Jo-Jo said, 'Look, rich man, it's all right for you to come here to New York and talk big about God changing lives. You've got new shoes and you've got a suit of clothes that match. Look at me! I'm a bum. There are ten kids in my family. We're on relief. They kicked me out – there wasn't enough food to go around.'

Jo-Jo was right. Then and there, on the public park bench, I took off my shoes and asked him to try them on.

'What's the gimmick? What are you trying to prove? That you got heart, or something? I'm not going to put your stinking shoes on.'

'You've been griping about shoes. Put them on.'

Jo-Jo said, 'I ain't never had new shoes.'

'Put them on.'

So, sullenly, Jo-Jo put on the shoes.

Then I got up and walked away. I walked down the street in my stocking feet, about two blocks, to the car. It was quite a circus, people looking and laughing, and just as I got to the car, Little Jo-Jo came up behind me and said, 'You forgot your shoes.'

'They're your shoes.' I got in the car.

'Preacher,' Jo-Jo said, reaching inside the open window, 'I forgot to shake your hand.'

So we shook. Then I said, 'Look. You don't have any place to live. I'm bumming a bed myself right now. But there's a couch out in the living room. Maybe the folks who took me in will take you in too. Let's go ask them.'

'Okay,' said Jo-Jo, just like that.

'Mrs Ortez,' I said, a little hesitantly, 'this is the President of the Coney Island Dragons. Jo-Jo, I'd like you to meet the lady who is putting me up for a while since I can't afford any place to sleep, just like you.'

Then I asked Mrs Ortez if Jo-Jo could stay with me a few days in her home. She looked at her two little children and she looked at the switchblade sticking out of Jo-Jo's pocket, and she very kindly went over and put her arm around him and said:

'Jo-Jo, you can sleep on the couch.'

It was a brave thing, as anyone knows who has worked with these potentially violent boys. I took Jo-Jo aside and said, 'Your clothes stink. We're in a home now, and we're going to have to do something. I've got eight dollars. We'll go to an Army-Navy store and get you a shirt and a pair of trousers.'

So I put on my old pair of shoes and took Jo-Jo downstairs and into the nearest Army-Navy store we could find. He went into the back room of the store to change and simply left his old clothes where he stepped out of them. On the way back home, Jo-Jo looked at his reflection in every store window. 'Not bad ... not bad,' he said over and over.

So far, what I'd done with Jo-Jo was similar to what any social agency might have done. And it was no doubt a good thing that this boy at last had a pair of shoes and a shirt, and that that night he didn't have to sleep in the subway. But at heart, Jo-Jo was very much the same boy.

It took a change in me to bring about a change in Jo-Jo. And this change has affected both our lives ever since.

That evening at St Nick's was as bad as ever. There was the usual breaking up, laughing, jeering. There was the usual first fights and threats. There were the same suggestive gestures on the part of the girls, and the same lewd responses on the part of the boys. Jo-Jo was there, watching it all. He came out of curiosity, but he wanted me to know that he thought the whole thing was a lot of rot.

Afterwards, on the way back to the Ortez apartment I was silent. I'd been hurt by the lack of response, and actually, behind the wheel of the car, I was sulking.

'Preach, you're trying too hard.'

It came just like that. Without warning, and from a homeless boy who pretended to be calloused through and through, came a penetrating, wonderful piece of insight.

The impact of those words was immense. They went through me as if they had been spoken by God Himself. I turned to stare at Jo-Jo so abruptly he thought I was angry, and raised his arm in defence.

Of course! *I* had been out there trying to change lives; I wasn't bringing the Holy Spirit to the gangs. I was bringing Dave Wilkerson. Even in giving Jo-Jo a pair of shoes *I* had been out in front. I knew in that moment that I would never be able to help Jo-Jo. I would never be able to help the gangs. All I could do was make an introduction, then step aside.

'You're trying too hard.' The sudden insight brought a great burst of laughter which seemed to unsettle Jo-Jo.

'Cut it out, Preacher.'

'I'm laughing, Jo-Jo, because you've helped me. From now on I'm not going to try so hard. I'm going to step aside and let the Spirit come through.'

Jo-Jo was silent for a while. He cocked his head.

'I don't feel nothing,' he said. 'Nothing at all. I don't expect to feel nothing, either.'

We didn't speak again until we got upstairs to the Ortez apartment. Then suddenly again, with that direct way he has, Little Jo-Jo was making me a deal.

'Look, Davie, you got a kid coming, right?'

I had told Jo-Jo that Gwen would be going to the hospital. The baby might be born any time.

'And you say there is a God and He loves me, right?'

'That's right,' I said.

'All right, if there is a God, and if I pray to Him, He'll hear my prayers, right?'

'Absolutely.'

'All right. What do you want, a boy or a girl?'

I could see the trap coming, but I didn't know what to do about it. 'Now look, Jo-Jo, prayer isn't a slot machine where you put the right coin in and out comes the candy.'

'In other words you're not so sure about this God business either.'

'I didn't say that at all.'

'What do you want? Boy or girl?'

I admitted that since we already had two girls we were hoping for a boy. Little Jo-Jo listened. Then he did a thing which was as hard for him as it was for Moses to strike the stone in the desert and ask water to come out. Little Jo-Jo said a prayer.

'Now God, if You are up there and if You love me, give this preacher a boy.'

That was Jo-Jo's prayer. It was a real one, and when he finished he was blinking hard. I was flabbergasted. I ran into my bare little bedroom and I began to pray as I hadn't prayed since I'd been in New York.

Jo-Jo and the Ortezes were sound asleep when the telephone call came, at 2:30 that night. I was still praying. I went out to the phone.

It was my mother-in-law. 'David!' she said. 'I couldn't wait until morning to call. I just had to tell you that you're a father!'

I couldn't bring myself to ask the question.

'David. David? Are you there?'

'I'm here.'

'Don't you want to know whether it was a boy or a girl?'

'More than you know.'

'David, you've got a great big, strapping, ten-pound son.'

Of course the skeptics will point out that there was a fifty-fifty chance of Little Jo-Jo's prayer coming true, just statistically. But something else was going on that night, something too deep for statistics. When I went in and woke Jo-Jo up with the news he scratched his head.

'What do you know?' he said. 'What do you know about that! What do you know ...'

Before the night was over, Jo-Jo was a changed boy. It began with tears; Jo-Jo cried the bitterness out and he cried the hatred out. He cried out the doubts and the fears too. And when he was all through there was room for the kind of love the Christian knows, which doesn't depend on parents or preachers or even upon prayers being answered in the way we think they should be answered. From that day on, Jo-Jo had a love that was his for always, and he had taught me a lesson that was mine for always.

We humans can work hard for each other, and we should and we must work. But it is God, and only God, who heals.

Chapter Ten

It was almost time for the meeting to begin. The auditorium was filling up on this final night of the rally. Far more young people had already come than had come on any previous evening. I saw some of the Chaplains; I saw the Dragons, and some GGIs. Among them, I was interested to note, was Maria.

But nowhere could I see a Mau Mau, although I looked everywhere for the bright red jackets with the big double M.

I hadn't been able to forget the appealing face and open manner of Israel, president of the Mau Maus. I'd been down to invite this gang to the rally as my personal guests, and to tell them about the special bus that we'd hired for them. When I said that I would reserve some seats down front just for them, Israel promised to come and bring the others.

But it was the last night and they weren't here, and I thought I knew why. Nicky. He had stood seething and silent while Israel and I talked, exuding hatred for me and everything I stood for.

I wandered to a window overlooking the street. A bus was arriving. I knew it was the Mau Maus even before I saw them. I knew by the way the bus pulled into the kerb: it nosed in fast, as if the driver couldn't wait to get rid of his passengers. The doors opened fore and aft and spilled out nearly fifty teenagers, shouting and shoving and out for a ball. One boy tossed away an empty bottle of wine as he stepped down. In the short distance between the bus stop and the arena entrance, they

picked up several teen-age girls who were standing around outside in very brief shorts and halters.

'Lord,' I said aloud, 'what have I gotten into?'

I'd asked the ushers to reserve the first three rows in the
arena but had not revealed who the seats were for. Now the
head usher came rushing up to me, excited and upset.

'Reverend, I don't know what to do.' He drew me out
onto the balcony and pointed down into the arena, where Israel
and Nicky were tapping their way down the aisle with their
canes, whistling and jeering as they came. 'Those are Mau
Maus,' the head usher said. 'I don't think I can keep them out
of those reserved seats.'

'That's all right,' I said. 'They're who the seats are for.
Those are friends of mine.'

But I sounded more confident than I felt. I left the usher
blinking and staring after me and hurried downstairs to the dressing rooms. There I found an atmosphere of grave foreboding. 'I
don't like the looks of it,' said the manager of the arena. 'There
are rival gangs out there, and we could have a full-scale rumble
on our hands.'

'Do you think we ought to call more police, just in
case?' asked one of the ministers who knew the gangs.

I looked out again. One of our own teen-age girls, a
remarkable young singer, as pretty as a movie star, was walking
onto the centre of the stage which had been set up at one end of
the arena.

'Let's see how Mary does,' I said. 'Maybe we won't have
to call more police. Maybe we can soothe the savage beast with
song.'

But as Mary Arguinzoni began to sing, the hollering and
whistling doubled.

'Hey, babe! Watch out for the curves!'

'You got time after the show for a poor old sinner?'

'What's your name, honey?'

The boys were standing on their seats doing the Fish, and the girls in their halters and too-brief briefs gyrated to the gospel song that Mary sang. She looked over to where I was standing in the wings and asked with her eyes what she should do. Despite the cheers and the clapping and the calls for another song, I signalled to Mary that she should come away.

'Do you want to call the thing off, Dave?'

'No. Not yet. Let's wait just a little longer. I'm going to try to talk to them. If you see things aren't going right, then you can do whatever you choose.'

I walked out. It was a long walk to the centre of the stage. And of course Israel had to let me know he was there.

'Hey, Davie! Here I am. I told you I'd come and bring my boys.'

I turned to smile at him, and my eyes met the rock-hard gaze of Nicky. Then I had a sudden inspiration.

'We're going to do something different tonight,' I announced over the loud-speaker system. 'We're going to ask the gang members themselves to take up the collection.' I looked right at Nicky as I spoke. 'May I have six volunteers?'

Nicky was on his feet in a flash, incredulity and secret triumph struggling on his face. He pointed at five Mau Maus and the six of them came forward and lined up in front of the stage. One good result of my decision was apparent already: that arena had come to attention. Hundreds of teenagers stopped their cavorting and leaned forward in breathless anticipation.

I stepped to the wings and took the paper milk-shake cartons from the hands of the astonished ushers. 'Now,' I said to the boys as I handed them round, 'when you've passed down the aisles, I'd like you to bring the offerings around behind that curtain and up onto the stage.' I pointed to the place, watching Nicky's face. Behind that curtain, as well as the stage steps, there was a door to the street. A big arrow announced it: EXIT. Nicky accepted the carton solemnly, but in his eyes I could read mockery and contempt.

And so while the organ played, Nicky and his boys took up the collection. He did well as a fund-raiser, too. Nicky had sixteen stabbings to his record and was known as a vicious knife-fighter not only to the Brooklyn kids but to the gangs in Manhattan and the Bronx as well. He was also famous for his baseball-bat tactics. Newspapers had pegged him 'The Garbage-Can Fighter' because in a rumble he would put a can over his head and wade into battle swinging his bat blindly in a deadly circle. When Nicky stood at the end of a row, shaking his carton, the kids dug deep.

When he was satisfied that he had enough, he signalled the other boys and together they walked down front and ducked behind the curtain. I waited, standing on the stage.

A wave of giggles swept over the room. A minute passed. Girls clapped their hands to their mouths to keep in the glee. Two minutes. Now the suppressed laughter exploded in guffaws, and my inspiration evaporated into sheerest lunacy before my eyes. The kids were on their feet, stamping and howling in derision.

Then the room froze. I turned my head. Nicky and the others were crossing the stage toward me, the full cartons in their hands. Nicky looked at me with bewildered, almost frightened eyes, as though he himself could not understand what he was doing.

'Here's your money, Preacher,' he said – not graciously – angrily, relunctantly, as though the words were dragged out of him.

'Thank you, Nicky,' I said, in what I hoped was a casual voice. I walked over to the pulpit as though I had not just lived through the worst two minutes of my life.

There was not a sound in the room as the six boys filed slowly back to their places. I began to speak, my heart beating high with hope. But if I thought I had won the sympathy of that crowd for my message, I was sorely mistaken. I had gotten their ears, but I couldn't seem to get near their hearts.

I couldn't understand what was wrong with my sermon. I'd done everything I could to make it a good one. I'd spent hours preparing it, and prayed over every line of it. I'd even fasted in the hope that this would strengthen my delivery and my persuasiveness. But I might as well have stood up and read the stock-market report. Nothing I said seemed real to these kids; nothing came through to them. I preached for perhaps fifteen minutes, and all I could sense was the growing restlessness of the crowd. I had reached the point in the sermon where I quoted Jesus' command to love one another.

Suddenly someone jumped up in the second row. He stood on his chair and shouted:

'Hold on, Preacher! Hold on! You say you want me to love them Dagoes? One of them cut me with a razor. I'll love them all right – with a lead pipe.'

And another boy, this one from the Hell Burners' section, jumped up and ripped open his shirt.

'I got a bullet hole here, Preacher. One of them Nigger gangs did it. And you say we're supposed to love them? Man, you're not real.'

It didn't sound real, not in that room so charged with hatred. It didn't sound humanly possible. 'It isn't anything we can achieve through our own efforts,' I admitted. 'This is God's love I'm talking about. We simply have to ask Him to give us His kind of love. We cannot work it up by ourselves.'

And then, suddenly, with brilliant clarity, I saw that these words were intended for myself. Wasn't this the very lesson I'd learned from Jo-Jo? There's very little we humans can do to change ourselves or others, to heal them, to fill them with love instead of hate. We can bring our hearts and minds to God, but then we must leave them there.

I bowed my head, as I had done on the street.

Right there I turned the meeting over. 'All right, Jesus,' I prayed, 'there is nothing more that I can do. I invited these young people here, now I'm going to step out of the picture.

Come, Holy Spirit. If you want to reach the hearts of any of these boys and girls, it will have to be through Your presence. Have Your own way, Lord. Have Your own way.'

Three minutes can be an incredibly long period of time. I stood before that crowd with my head bowed for three minutes. I did not say a word. I did not move. I prayed, quietly and yieldingly. It didn't bother me any more that some of the kids were laughing. Nor did it surprise me when slowly the great hall began to quiet down. First it was the front three rows. I recognized Israel's voice: 'All right, you guys! Can it.'

The quiet spread backwards through the house, and up to the balconies. Before the three minutes were up, that prize-fight arena was totally silent.

And then I heard the sound of someone crying.

I opened my eyes. In the front row Israel was tugging at a handkerchief in his hip pocket. He pulled it out and blew his nose very loudly, then blinked and sniffed.

I continued praying, 'Lord, sweep over this whole group.'

And while I prayed, Nicky got out his handkerchief. I couldn't believe my eyes and took another look. There he was, leaning on his cane, snorting and blinking and angry with himself for crying. One of the boys put a hand on his shoulder. Nicky shrugged him off.

I knew the time had come to speak out. In a loud voice I said:

'All right. You've felt Him; He's here; He's in this room, come especially for you. If you want to have your life changed, now is the time. Stand up and come forward!'

Israel didn't hesitate. He stood up and faced his gang. 'Boys,' he said, 'I've been your leader for three years. When I say go, you go! Right?'

'Right!' said the Mau Maus.

'Well, I'm going forward now and you're coming along. Get on your feet!'

They jumped up as a man, and followed Israel forward. No, they raced him elbowing each other to get there first. I looked to see if Nicky was among them. He was.

The surge forward was contagious. More than thirty boys from other gangs followed the Mau Maus downstairs to the dressing room where workers from the churches were ready. We were swamped. I kept going from room to room, trying to help where I could, and it was during one of these tours that I suddenly realized a peculiar thing. There were dozens of boys who had come forward for this new life, and only three girls. I heard a whistle out in the hall, and poked my head through the door just in time to see one of the other girls open her blouse, expose a bare breast and call to the boys from her neighbourhood. 'You go in there and you won't get this.'

Before we could stop them, other girls had picked up the theme and succeeded in drawing a few of the boys away. It was a puzzling thing. I suppose the girls, hearing us talk about love, felt a simple jealousy. They didn't want to share love with anybody, and were fighting in the only way they knew to hold on to the little, poor, shoddy shreds of 'love' that they did have.

The conversion hardest for me to believe was Nicky's.

There he stood, a great grin on his face, saying in his strained, stammering way, 'I am giving my heart to God, Davie.'

I couldn't believe him. The change was too sudden. He was puffing his perpetual cigarette, the little jets of smoke streaming out the side of his mouth, telling me that something new had happened in his heart. What about the narcotics addiction? What about the stealing and the mugging, the heavy drinking, the stabbings and the sadism? Nicky must have read my thoughts, because he defended himself by the only technique he knew, cursing:

'Damn it, Davie, I've given my heart to God.'

'All right, Nicky, okay.' I wanted to do something to give

him confidence, so I asked him and Israel to come with me, and I found them, and each of the Mau Maus who had come forward, copies of the Bible. There were two sizes, little pocket editions and much larger ones. The boys didn't want the little ones.

'Give us them big books, Davie, so people can see what we're carrying.'

And with that, most of the boys lit up cigarettes, tucked their Bibles under their arms, and walked out.

It was early the next morning that the phone call came. Mrs Ortez stuck her head in the door of my little room. 'Davie, it's the police on the phone.'

'The police!'

My heart sank. And when I stumbled out to the phone, the words I heard didn't make me feel any better. The lieutenant asked me if I knew the Mau Mau gang, and when I said that I did, he asked if I'd come right down.

When I got to the Edward Street Precinct, sure enough, there were half-a-dozen boys from the gang. I walked past them briskly and introduced myself at the desk. What happened next I shall never forget.

The desk sergeant called the lieutenant, and the lieutenant assembled the whole force. The lieutenant stuck out his hand.

'Reverend,' he said, 'I want to shake your hand.' I took his offer, and he pumped me firmly.

'How did you do it?' he asked. 'These boys declared war on us a few months ago. They've given us nothing but trouble for years. Then this morning they all troop in here and you know what they want?'

I shook my head.

'They want us to autograph their Bibles!'

I looked at Nicky and Israel and the boys who were with them. They grinned at me.

'Any time we can help you set up another street meeting, Reverend, just let us know,' said the lieutenant, and as we all stepped out onto the sidewalks of Brooklyn, I saw the sergeant sitting at his desk, shaking his head in wonder.

The boys, I learned, had been reading their Bibles most of the night. They were fascinated with the Old Testament stories particularly.

'Davie!' said Israel, 'I'm in the Bible! Look, here's my name all over the place.'

That night when I called Gwen at the hospital I was so full of the meetings I could hardly talk of anything else. 'Last night made everything worthwhile honey,' I told her. 'If only you could have been here!'

'Well, I've been kind of busy, Dave,' she said. 'Remind me to tell you about it sometime – when you get back to earth, that is.'

Chapter Eleven

I made the transition from the sweltering streets of New York to the coolness of the Pennsylvania hills in one swift turnpike jump. I should have enjoyed the contrast. But every mile along the way I was thinking about Buckboard and Stagecoach, Nicky and Israel, Maria and Jo-Jo and Angelo: boys and girls whose lives had become so strangely entwined in my own.

It was the same thing back in Philipsburg. I sat in the shade of our backyard, sipping the orangeade Gwen had made for me, watching my baby son in his basket under the trees. And I caught my mind slipping back to kids in New York, fighting for the right to sit in one sweaty corner of a public park.

'Your parish is Philipsburg,' Gwen reminded me gently one night, when I'd worried aloud for half an hour about Angelo Morales who had made up his mind to be a preacher but had no money for school. 'You mustn't neglect your own church.'

Gwen was right, of course, and for the next six months I poured everything I had into my mountain parish. It was satisfying work and I loved it, but the other place was never very far from my thoughts.

'I've noticed,' one of my parishioners told me, 'you never get quite as excited about things here as you do about those kids in the city.'

I swallowed. I hadn't thought it showed.

But show it or not, I was getting trickles of an idea which alarmed me: that I take my family and move to New

York as a full-time servant to these boys. Maybe I could never get them their house, but I could work with them on the street.

The idea was persistent with me. I pondered it through as I drove over the countryside that fall and winter on pastoral visits. I preached sermons on Knowing God's Will, hoping to learn something about how to get guidance.

But most of all I thought about it on a certain hilltop. Ever since I was a boy I have taken my deepest perplexities to the hills. One in particular heard my complaints as a child: Old Baldy, a nobby little mountain near our home in Barnesboro, Pennsylvania.

From Old Baldy, I could look down on our house and watch Mother and Dad and the other children running around the neighbourhood trying to find me. Sometimes I would stay up there for the better part of a day, thinking through the problems a boy has to conquer. When I got back, I always got a licking, but Dad's switch never kept me from making my journey again, because up there I found an aloofness and a detachment that I needed.

And I needed it badly now, too. Not far from our church there was an abandoned strip mine. I chose this spot for my adult version of Old Baldy. I could see the church from this hill, and if I parked the car in a certain spot, Gwen could see it and not worry about me when I was gone for a long time.

Up there on my hill, I considered the matter. Was it possible, I wondered, that this urging to go to New York came from God? Was I truly supposed to abandon this parish and move Gwen and our three small children into the dirty city with all its problems for daily living?

A definite and clear answer did not come right away. Like most guidance, it came to me one step at a time.

The first step was a return visit to New York.

'Do you realize that a year has passed since I was thrown out of the Farmer trial?' I asked Gwen one February morning.

'Uh, oh!' said Gwen.

'What do you mean by that?'

'You're getting ready to go back to New York, aren't you?'

I laughed. 'Well, I had been thinking of a very brief visit. Just overnight.'

'Mm hm.'

It felt good to drive over the George Washington Bridge again, and later over the Brooklyn Bridge. It was good to walk through the streets again, jumping over piles of snow as I had done when I first came to the city. I was surprised at how much at home I felt. I wanted to look up old friends. I wanted to revisit sites where miracles had happened in the hearts of boys.

One of these sites was the Fort Greene Projects. I was walking down the street, reliving the scene Jimmy Stahl and I had enacted there, when suddenly I heard my name called.

'Davie! Preacher!'

I turned and saw two fine-looking Negro soldiers approaching me at a run. They were wearing neat, freshly pressed uniforms and their shoes shone till it hurt the eye.

I stared at them. 'Buckboard! Stagecoach!' I hardly recognized them: they must have put on twenty pounds each.

'Yessir,' they said together, coming to a snappy attention. 'Look good, eh Davie?'

Getting into the Army is a kind of ultimate for many boys from the housing projects. The literacy and health requirements are stiff enough so that it is considered a Certificate of Worth to be able to wear a uniform. Buckboard, Stagecoach and I had a great reunion. They told me they were doing real well. They told me they quit the gang after our street meeting and never went back.

'In fact, Preach,' said Stagecoach, 'the Chaplain gang broke up for the rest of the summer. Nobody felt like fighting.'

I left Buckboard and Stagecoach with real regret. I was surprised at the strength of my own reactions to this unexpected meeting. I had liked these boys and missed them more than I had known.

But the great surprise was ahead for me.

I set out down Edward Street, past the lamp post where Jimmy and I had preached, looking for Israel and Nicky. I saw a young Spanish lad I thought I recognized and asked him if he knew the whereabouts of Nicky and Israel of the Mau Maus.

The boy looked at me oddly. 'You mean those jitter-buggers who turned saints?' He meant it as a joke but my heart leaped. 'Glory to God!' I thought. 'They're holding on!'

But the next piece of news left me reeling. Not only were they holding on, but Nicky, at any rate, was going places.

'Nicky, huh!' said the boy with a disdainful snort. 'He's crazy. He's going to be one of these nutty preachers.'

I stood on the street with my mouth hanging open. 'Did I hear you right? Nicky wants to become a *preacher?*'

'That's what he says.'

Where could I find him, I wanted to know. When had he talked about preaching? Who had he talked to? Had he taken any first steps? The boy couldn't answer me, so I took off and looked for Nicky myself.

I found him a little later, sitting on some apartment-house steps and talking to another boy.

'Nicky?' I said.

Nicky turned around, and I stared into a face I didn't know. Where the hard, defensive exterior had been, there was openness and animation, a charming and eager boy's face. Now his eyes lit up with real joy.

'Preacher!' He hopped up and ran toward me. 'Davie!' He turned to the boy who was with him. 'Look, man! This is the preacher I told you about. This is the one who bugged me.'

It was wonderful to see him. After introductions and polite talk, I asked Nicky if it was true that he wanted to go into the ministry.

Nicky looked down at the sidewalk. 'I never wanted anything so bad, Davie,' he said.

'This is just terrific news!' I said. 'Tell me, have you done anything about it yet?'

'I don't know how to start.'

I was overflowing with ideas. I offered to write to some theological schools. I wanted to sponsor him myself. I wanted him to go to a voice clinic for his impeded speech. I even had some thoughts about raising the necessary money for all this. I had been invited to speak to a church group in Elmira, New York, a few weeks from then, on the problems of young people in the cities. It struck me as ironic that in that same city, Luis Alvarez had been imprisoned. The boys don't stay long in Elmira. Luis would be transferred by now; I had no idea where he was.

'Nicky,' I said, 'will you come with me to Elmira? Will you tell your story to the people there? It could be that they'll be able to help you.'

I had no sooner made the suggestion than I began to have qualms about it. Nicky's story, as it had come to me in bits and pieces, was an exceedingly ugly one, full of a brutality and a strange irrationality that might be well-nigh incomprehensible in Elmira, New York. I was accustomed by now to chilling sights and sounds on New York's streets, and even I found his story shocking.

Still, I argued with myself, the Elmira church had expressed a desire to learn about the gangs: here indeed would be a speedy introduction. For me it would mean a chance to hear Nicky's story from start to finish as I had not yet done, and best of all, a chance to see the St Nick experience from the other side.

———————

So that was how Nicky came to be standing on a platform in Elmira, New York, a few weeks later, to relate the story of his life. I had spent some time on his introduction, stressing the poverty and loneliness that spawned boys like this so that the audience would not judge him too harshly before they heard him through.

My precautions were unnecessary. From the moment he began to speak, that roomful of people was with him. His

own words, the pathetic narrowness of his experience – for all
he was so knowing – the flat, staccato recital by a boy who had
not learned to exaggerate or embellish, told more than volumes
of sociology about the world he came from.

'I was mostly in the streets,' he began, 'because my parents had customers coming where we lived. They would come
at night or in the day and then all of us kids had to go out. They
were spiritualists, my parents. They advertised in the Spanish
papers that they would talk with the dead and cure sickness, and
they would also give advice about money and family problems.

'There was only one room at home, so us kids were in
the street. At first the other kids beat me up and I was afraid all
the time. Then I learned how to fight and they were scared of me
and they left me alone. After a while I got so I liked it better in
the street than I did at home. At home I was the youngest one.
I was nothing. But in the street they knew who I was.

'My family moved a lot and mostly it was on account
of me. If there was any trouble the police would come around
asking questions and then the superintendent wherever we
lived would go to my parents and say we had to move. They
didn't want their building to have trouble with the police. It was
that way if the police just asked a Puerto Rican boy a question.
It didn't matter if he did anything, the minute the police came
around asking about him, he and his family had to get out.

'I didn't know why I acted like I did. There was a thing
inside me that scared me. It worried me all the time but I couldn't
stop it. It was this feeling I got if I saw a cripple. It was a feeling
like I wanted to kill him. It was that way with blind people, too,
or real little kids – anyone weak or hurt – I would hate them.

'One day I told my old man about this thing. We never
talked or anything but this thing scared me. So I told him and
he said I had a devil. He tried to call the devil out of me, but it
wouldn't come.

'The crazy thing in me got worse and worse. If someone
had crutches I would kick them or if an old man had a beard I

would try to pull it out and I would rough up little kids. And all the while I would be scared and wanting to cry, but the thing inside me was laughing and laughing. The other thing was blood. The minute I saw blood I would begin to laugh and I couldn't stop it.

'When we moved into the Fort Greene Projects, I went in with the Mau Maus. They wanted me to be President. But in a rumble the President has to direct traffic (give orders) and I wanted to fight. So they made me Vice-President.

'I was also Sergeant-at-Arms. That meant I was in charge of the arsenal. We had garrison belts and bayonets and switch-blades and zip guns. I liked to go in and just look at those things. You steal a car aerial to make the zip guns. You use a door latch for the trip hammer and they shoot .22 shells.

'But for rumbling I liked a baseball bat. I'd cut a hole in a garbage can to see out, then I'd put it over my head and swing the bat. The Mau Maus would never fight alongside me because when I got crazy like that I would beat on anybody.

'I also learned how to stick with a knife, which is when you cut someone but don't kill him. I stuck sixteen people, and I was in jail twelve times. Some of those times my picture was in the paper. When I walked down the street everyone knew me and the mothers would call their little kids.

'The gangs knew me too. One day when I was waiting for a subway five guys came up behind me. They got a leather belt around my neck and kept twisting it. I didn't die, but I used to wish I had because after that I could never talk right. There was a funny noise in my throat. I had this hate of people who had anything wrong with them, and now it was me. I had to bop all the time, after that, to keep respect.

'Our gang controlled the turf as far as Coney Island and Ralph Avenue. We had red jackets with MM on them and we wore continental heels, which are good in a fight. One day we were in a candy store on Flatbush Avenue. There were six of us, drinking soda, when seven Bishops walked in. The Bishop gang was at war with the Mau Maus.

'One of the Bishops went up to the candy counter like he owned it. My boys were watching me. I walked over and I shoved him. He shoved back and then everyone was fighting. The owner's wife started screaming. All the other customers ran out on the sidewalk. There was a butcher knife on the counter. One of my boys picked it up and cut a Bishop five times through the scalp. I saw the blood and I started to laugh. I knew he was dead and I was scared but I couldn't stop laughing. The owner's wife was telephoning the police. Another one of my boys picked up that butcher knife and hit her right in the stomach. Then we ran.

'I never touched the knife so I didn't go to jail. But my parents had to go to the court and I guess it was the first time they looked at me. They got scared when they saw what I was. They decided to get out of New York and go back to Puerto Rico. My brother and I went to the airport to say good-bye to them. On the way back from the airport in his car he gave me a .32 pistol. He said, "You're on your own, Nick."

'The first thing I had to do was find a place to sleep. I held up a guy with the gun and got ten dollars. I rented a room on Myrtle Avenue. I was sixteen then. That's how I lived after that, holding up guys for money or something to hock.

'During the day it was all right. I was with the gang. Whatever the President and I told them to do they would do. But at night, when I had to go into that room, it was terrible. I would think about the two dead people in the candy store. I would bang my head on the floor to stop thinking about them. I started waking up in the middle of the night, crying for my mother. We never talked, or anything, before she left, but suddenly I felt like she should come and take care of me.

'I turned eighteen in July, 1958. That month the Dragons from the Red Hook Projects killed one of our boys. We were going down on the subway to get one of them. That's gang law: if one Mau Mau dies, one Dragon dies. We were walking down Edward Street on our way to the subway station when we saw a police car stopped and a whole bunch of Chaplains hanging around. The Chaplains are the Nigger gang in Fort Greene. We had a treaty with them that we wouldn't fight and we would work together if another gang invaded us.

'It looked like action so we went over. The Chaplains were all standing around two guys I never seen, one had a bugle and the other was a real skinny guy. Then somebody brought an American flag and the police car drove away. All it was, the two guys wanted to hold a street meeting.

'As soon as the flag came the skinny guy got up on a chair, opened up a book, and this is what he read out of it:

> For God so loved the world that He gave His only begotten Son, that whosoever believeth in Him should not perish.

'"Now," the preacher said, "I'm going to talk to you about 'Whosoever,' 'Whosoever' means Negroes and Puerto Ricans, and especially it means gang members. Do you know that when they crucified Jesus they crucified gang members too? One on each side of Him ..."

'I'd had enough. I said, "Come on you guys, we got business."

'Not one of them moved. It was the first time they didn't follow me. Then I got scared and I called that preacher every filthy name I knew. He paid no attention, just kept on talking, a long time.

'And the next thing you knew the President of the Chaplains flopped down on his knees, right on Edward Street, and started crying. The Vice-President and two War Lords got down beside him and they cried. One thing I couldn't stand was crying. I was glad when the Chaplains left. I figured we would go too.

'But then this preacher comes up to Israel – he was President of the Mau Maus – and starts shaking his hand. I figured he was trying to bust us up and I went up and shoved the preacher. Israel stared at me like he'd never seen me before.

'So that preacher heads for me. "Nicky," he says, "I love you."

'No one in my life ever told me that. I didn't know what to do. "You come near me, preacher," I said, "I'll kill you!" And I meant it. Well, Israel and the preacher talked some more, but at last he left and I thought it was over. Only we never went after the Dragons.

'But later this preacher came back and he talked about this big meeting for gangs they were going to have up in Manhattan, and how we should come. "We'd like to come, Preach," says Israel, "but how we going to get through Chink town?" "I'll send a bus for you," says the preacher. So then Israel said we'll come.

'Well, I said, not me. I felt like I'd rather die than go to that meeting. But when the gang went it turned out I was with them. I was scared not to be with the gang. I figured I would fix his little prayer meeting for him. When we got there here were three rows of seats right down front roped off for us. That surprised me some. The preacher said he'd save us seats but I never figured he'd do it.

'A lady was playing the organ and I got the guys stamping and shouting for action. Then a little girl came out on the stage and began to sing. I whistled at her and everyone laughed. It was all going my way and I was feeling good.

'Finally the preacher came out and he said, "Before the message tonight we're going to take up a collection."

'Well I figured I saw his angle. I'd been wondering all along what was in this for him. Now I saw he was a money-grabber like everyone else.

'"We're going to ask the gang members themselves to take it up," he says. "They'll bring the money around behind this curtain and up onto the stage."

'I figured he didn't have any good sense: anyone could see there was a door back there!

'"May I have six volunteers?" he says.

'Man, I was on my feet in a second. I pointed out five of my boys and we piled down there quick. Here was my chance to make him look silly. He gave us cardboard cartons. I wanted to get started right away but he made us stand there while he reeled off a long blessing. I tried not to laugh.

'Well, we worked that whole arena. If I didn't like what someone put in, I just stood there till he gave some more. They all knew Nicky. Then we met down behind the curtain.

'There was the door. It was wide open. I could see street lights and I heard a water truck spraying the street. Back in the arena some of them were laughing. They knew what we were pulling. My boys were watching me, waiting the word to cut out.

'And I just stood there. I didn't know what it was; I had a funny feeling. Suddenly I knew what it was: that preacher trusted me. That never happened in my life before and I just stood there, my boys watching me.

'Inside, I could hear they were giving him a hard time. They were shouting and stamping and he having to stand there and face them, trusting me.

"'All right, you guys," I said. "We're going up on that stage."

'They looked at me like I wasn't right in my head, but they never argued. I was that kind of guy that the kids didn't argue with. We went up the stairs and you never heard a place get quiet so fast. We gave him the cartons. "Here's your money, Preacher," I said.

'He just took the money, not surprised or anything, like he knew all the time I'd bring it.

'Well, I went back to my seat and I was thinking harder than I ever thought before. He started talking and it was all about the Holy Spirit. The preacher said the Holy Spirit could get inside people and make them clean. He said it didn't matter what they'd done, the Holy Spirit could make them start new, like babies.

'Suddenly I wanted that so bad I couldn't stand it. It was as if I was seeing myself for the first time. All the filth and the hate and the foulness like pictures in front of my eyes.

'"You can be different!" he said. "Your life can be changed!"

'I wanted that, I needed that, but I knew it couldn't happen to me. The preacher told us to come forward if we wanted to be changed but I knew it was no use for me.

'Then Israel told us all to get up. "I'm President," he said, "and this whole gang is going up there!"

'I was the first one at the rail. I kneeled down and said the first prayer of my life and this was it: "Dear God, I'm the dirtiest sinner in New York. I don't think You want me. If You do want me, You can have me. As bad as I was before, I want to be that good for Jesus."

'Later the preacher gave me a Bible and then I went home wondering if the Holy Ghost was really inside me, and how I would know. The first thing that happened, when I went in my room and shut the door I didn't feel scared. I felt like I had company in the room – not God or anyone like that, but the way I'd feel if my mother came back. I had four pot sticks (marijuana cigarettes) in my pocket. I ripped them up and threw them out the window.

'The next day everyone was staring because word had gone around that Nicky had religion. But another thing happened that made me know it was real. Little kids would always run when they saw me, but on that day two little boys stared at me a minute and then they came right up to me. They wanted me to measure and see which one of them was taller – nothing important. Only I put my arms around them because I knew then I was different, even if it didn't show except to kids.

'Then, a few weeks later, a Dragon came up to me and he said, "Is it true you don't carry weapons any more?" I told him it was true, and he pulled a ten-inch knife and went for my chest. I threw my hand up and caught the knife there. I don't know why, but he ran, and I stood there, looking at the blood coming from my hand. I remembered how blood always made me go crazy, but that day it didn't. Words came into my mind that I had read in my Bible, "The blood of Jesus Christ cleanseth us from all sin." I ripped my shirt and tied up my hand and from that day blood never bothered me.'

———————

As Nicky talked, a hush fell over the room – the scarcely breathing silence that invariably attends a miracle. For we were witnessing a miracle – or hearing one – that night in Elmira, and as each of the listeners took it in, he caught his breath with the little gasp that sends the knowledge racing through the room.

Nicky's voice, the straining, painful, stammering voice in which he had begun his story, had altered as he spoke. Gradually the words came more readily, the sounds clearer, until he was speaking as distinctly and effortlessly as anyone in the room. Only now had Nicky himself realized it. He stood on the platform trembling, unable to go on, tears streaming down his face.

I never knew what had caused his speech problem, whether it was physical injury resulting from the strangling, or what doctors term an 'hysterical' affliction. Nicky, of course, never in his wildest fancies considered seeing a doctor about it. I only knew that, from that night on, his voice was healed.

That night, too, a collection was taken in Elmira which started Nicky on a long and remarkable journey.

Chapter Twelve

Isat in my brown leather chair in the study at Philipsburg looking back with satisfaction on the last few months. It was my old TV-watching time and it seemed to me that I had every reason for thanksgiving at the choice I had made. I had written the Latin American Bible Institute, La Puente, California, about Nicky's dream of the ministry. I made no bones about his past career and I acknowledged frankly that he had not been in his new life long enough to prove himself. Would they, I asked them, accept him as a student on probation?

They wrote back that they would. Not only that, but they found themselves so intrigued with this story of transformation in a boy from the streets that not long afterwards they invited Angelo Morales to come there to school too.

No, I reflected, there was no doubting it. Buckboard and Stagecoach doing well, Nicky and Angelo on their way to becoming ministers: everything I saw pointed to the joyous completion of a task I'd been called to assist in.

I was not allowed to rest in this erroneous equilibrium for long. In the spring of 1959 came news which pulled me to my feet again and put me back on the path I had imagined would be a short one. Israel was in jail.

And on no minor charge: he was in jail for murder.

I drove to New York to see Israel's mother.

'My boy, he was so good for a while,' said Israel's mother, rocking from side to side in her distress. 'He settle down and when school start he do his studies. But then the gang is start up again. Do you know what it is, the "draft", Mr Wilkerson?'

I did know what the draft was. When gangs were just starting, or when their ranks were depleted for one reason or another, any boy in the neighbourhood was subject to one of the most vicious inventions of the fighting gang. He was simply drafted. He was stopped on the street and told that as of that moment he was a gang member and was expected to take part in the rumbles and obey all gang orders.

If he refused?

First, a simple beating followed. If he still refused, his thumbs or an arm was broken. If he refused again, his life was threatened. No one who knows the gangs takes such a threat lightly; most boys join up. Israel was actually fired at a number of times before he went back to the gang.

'My boy he so scared,' said Israel's mother. 'He go back. One night there was a big fight. One of the other boys got killed. Nobody even tried to say that Israel was the one who shoot him. But he was with those killers, so they put him in jail.'

Israel's mother showed me a letter from him, much handled and spotted with tears. He said he was sorry about the tragedy for her sake. He didn't seem bitter. He talked about the day when he would be getting out. He even spoke about me, saying that he would be 'sad for the preacher, when he finds out. Tell Davie I'd like to hear from him.'

What could we have done? How could we have kept Israel out of jail? Would it have helped to have me nearer, to give advice and friendship? Would it have helped to take him away from this neighbourhood, away from the gang that drafted him and the life that poisoned him?

I asked Israel's mother this, and she shook her head, moaning a little with grief.

'Maybe,' she said. 'I don't know. My boy was good for a while. Then he went back. He wanted to be good. Help him, Mr Wilkerson.'

I promised her that I would do everything I could. To begin with, I said, I could at least send Israel some correspondence courses at the prison.

Night and day he was on my mind. I talked to Gwen about him. I found myself asking people at the church what they would have done for him where I failed. I wrote him, but found that he could not write back. He could write only to his immediate family. Even his correspondence courses had to be sent through the prison chaplain. By early summer, when our Pennsylvania fields had turned green again, Israel was more in my mind than ever. At every opportunity I went up to my mountain to pray for him.

Further I could find nothing to do. As I write this, Israel is still in jail, this favourite of all the boys I met, this one that I loved on sight. My sense of frustration is as torturing today as it was when I first realized my impotence in the face of his crime and his punishment. I am waiting, that is all.

But in the meantime, at each appropriate occasion, I told his story to others, asking them what might have been done differently. Time and again the same answer came back: follow up. The flaw was in allowing these boys to be converted, then abandoning them.

But to follow up meant to be on the scene.

Some sort of turning point in my life was at hand. And then it happened.

It was a hot August night, a year and a half after my first timorous trip to New York. I was standing in the pulpit at the Wednesday evening prayer service, when suddenly my hands began to tremble. The thermometer read eighty-five degrees but now I was shaking as if I had a chill. Instead of feeling troubled or sick, however, I felt a tremendous exhilaration. It was as if the Spirit of the Lord were drawing near, in that room.

I still don't know how I managed to get through the service. But before I knew it the congregation was filing out to go home. At 10:30 I closed up the church and left by the rear door. What happened next was quite simple, yet it was one of those vivid moments of truth that I shall never forget as long as I live.

I went out into the backyard of the church. The moon was shining with an unusual brilliance. It bathed the sleeping town in its cold and mysterious light; but there was one spot in particular that seemed illuminated. In back of the church there was a four-acre field which had been planted in grain. The wheat now stood about a foot and a half high. I found myself propelled into the very centre of this field of grain, swaying in the night breeze. And suddenly I was quoting to myself the biblical figure of the harvest: "'Look, I tell you," said Jesus, "look round on the fields; they are already white, ripe for harvest. The reaper is drawing his pay and gathering a crop for eternal life, so that sower and reaper may rejoice together. That is how the saying comes true: One sows and another reaps. I sent you to reap a crop for which you have not toiled. Others toiled and you have come in for the harvest of their toil.'"[1]

In my mind's eye I saw each of the blades of wheat as a youngster on the streets of the city, hungry for a new beginning. And then I turned and looked at the church and the parsonage where Gwen and the three children were, safe, happy, secure in their life in a country parish. But as I stood and looked at them, a quiet inner voice spoke to me as clearly as if a friend had been standing nearby. 'The church is no longer yours,' I was told. 'You are to leave.'

I looked at the parsonage, and the same inner voice said, 'This home is no longer yours. You are to leave.'

And, in the same still, slow and inner voice I answered, 'Yes, Lord. I shall go.'

I walked over to the parsonage after that, and there was Gwen, waiting up. She was dressed for bed, but I could tell from looking at her that something had been happening to her too.

---

[1]John 4:35-38 (New English Bible)

'What is it, Gwen?'

'How do you mean?'

'There's something different about you.'

'David,' Gwen said, 'you don't have to tell me. I know already. You're going to leave the church, aren't you? You've got to leave.'

I looked at Gwen a long time before I answered her. In the moonlight that flowed into the parsonage bedroom, I could see the glint of a tear in the corner of her eye.

'I heard it too, David,' said Gwen. 'We're going, aren't we?'

In the darkness I put my arms around her. 'Yes, my dear one. We're going.'

────────

The following Sunday was our fifth anniversary as pastor-and-family at the Philipsburg church.

I stood in the pulpit that morning and looked out at the faces of the people we knew so well.

'My friends,' I said, 'you are probably expecting me to give you an anniversary message.

'As you know, these have been five extraordinarily happy and wonderful years for me, for my wife, and for our children. Two of our babies were born here in Philipsburg. We will always remember these years as a special time of close friendship.

'But an unusual thing happened last Wednesday night – something which can have but one explanation.'

I then told the congregation of my experience in the grain field, and of Gwen's amazing parallel experience inside the parsonage. I told them that I did not doubt this to be the voice of the Lord, and that we would have to obey. I couldn't answer their questions about where we would go. I suspected it would be New York, but I wasn't sure. All I knew was that we were to leave Philipsburg: now, without delay.

What an amazing thing it is to live this life of the Spirit! That very afternoon when I returned to the parsonage, the telephone began to ring. One call was from Florida, from a pastor who said that he couldn't shake the strong urging to telephone me and invite me to come and conduct a series of retreat meetings for him immediately. Another call came, then another, and before the day was over I found myself booked for twelve weeks of speaking engagements around the country. Within three weeks we had stored our furniture and moved from the parsonage into four rooms in my wife's parents' house.

And then I took off. For the rest of that summer and for part of the next winter, too, I held meetings in various cities and towns across the nation. I had to laugh at myself: I measured the distance to each new place not from where I happened to be at the moment but from New York City. The town drew me like a lodestone. Whenever possible I chose engagements that would take me near the huge, congested, anguish-filled city that I loved in such a special way.

In the dead of winter, 1960, one of these engagements took me to Irvington, New Jersey. I stayed there with a pastor named Reginald Yake, and I told him, as I told everyone, about some of the experiences I had had in New York. Mr Yake sat on the arm of his sofa for an hour, listening intently and asking questions.

'Dave,' he said at last, 'it seems to me that the churches need a full-time worker among the gangs in New York. I wonder whether you would let me make a few telephone calls to some friends in the city.'

One of the men he called was Stanley Berg, co-pastor of Glad Tidings Tabernacle on West 33rd Street, near Penn Station. A meeting of interested clergymen was scheduled in the basement of Mr Berg's church.

It was an ordinary enough meeting. Someone read a letter from Police Commissioner Kennedy urging the churches to take a more vigorous stand in matters affecting young people. Mr Berg stood up and spoke a little about the work I had already been doing. Then I got up and talked about the direction in which I thought work among teen-agers might now go.

Before we were through, a new ministry was born. Since its main purpose was to reach young boys and girls with the message of God's love, we called the new ministry Teen-Age Evangelism. I had already been involved in this work, so I was voted director of the infant organization. A Police Captain named Paul DiLena, a member of Mr Berg's church, was voted secretary-treasurer. Poor Paul: he wasn't at the meeting to defend himself.

Next came the question of money. That was handled very simply. We figured that for office space, printing, salaries and so forth, a budget of $20,000 would be minimal. So we gave ourselves a budget of $20,000. Of course, there was no actual *cash* represented, as our Secretary-Treasurer discovered a few moments later when Stanley Berg called him to inform him of his victory at the polls.

'Paul,' said Pastor Berg, 'there's good news. You have just been elected Treasurer of Teen-Age Evangelism. David Wilkerson is your Director in this fight for young people. And you'll be glad to hear that you've got a budget of $20,000 for the first year.'

Captain DiLena said, 'Who is David Wilkerson, who's got the books, and where is the money?'

'Paul,' said Pastor Berg, 'we have no books, we have no money, and Dave Wilkerson is a preacher from the hills of Pennsylvania who believes he belongs in New York.'

Paul laughed. 'You make it sound naïve,' he said.

'We are naïve, Paul,' said Pastor Berg. 'Just about as naïve as David was when he stepped up to Goliath with nothing but a sling, a pebble ... and the conviction that he was on God's side.'

Chapter Thirteen

It was a blustering, gray February morning, almost exactly two years from that other February day when I sold the television set and found myself launched on this strange adventure.

I was standing inside the glass doors on the Staten Island ferry, hardly realizing myself what a giant stride we had just made toward my dream. Spume splashed up on the deck from a choppy sea. Off the starboard was the Statue of Liberty, and I found myself thinking how appropriate it was that I would pass here each morning. Because I was going to Staten Island on a specific and hopeful mission: to rent offices for our new programme aimed at setting youngsters free.

I had an address in my pocket which sounded appropriate too: 1865 Victory Boulevard. This had been suggested as the site of our headquarters suite. But when I got to this 'headquarters suite' I had to smile. It consisted of three rather grubby rooms in a less-than-chic neighbourhood. There was an outer office, an inner office and a shipping room.

'Well, Lord,' I said, 'I'm really grateful this isn't fancy. I wouldn't know how to act in a fancy place.'

Teen-Age Evangelism got its start in these three rooms. We had one paid employee: myself. And I didn't receive enough salary to afford even the cheapest room in the cheapest boarding house. I set up a couch next to my desk in the middle office. I ate what I could cook on a hot plate or, on special occasions, with friends around New York who would look at my slender frame and ask me to share a meal with them.

But the part of the arrangement that was hardest was having the family divided. Gwen remained in Pittsburgh with her folks, and she longed to join me at the earliest moment.

'I know what you're doing is right, Dave,' she said on one of our visits-by-telephone. 'But I'm lonesome. Gary's growing up without even knowing what you look like.'

We agreed that we would move the family to New York as soon as the school year was over for Bonnie and Debbie, even if it meant sleeping on a park bench. But in the meantime, I found certain advantages in my monastic existence. My little cell of a home was a perfect place for prayer. There were no physical comforts to offer distraction. The ten-by-twelve room had just one desk, a hard straight-backed chair, and my couch. I found that it was a pleasure to pray in this setting of austerity, and each night I looked forward to my old television-viewing time – midnight to two a.m. – as a time of renewal. Never did I get up without being refreshed, encouraged and filled with new enthusiasm.

Those early days were exciting. The Spanish- and English-speaking Assemblies churches in the New York area had supplied me with $1,000 to launch our work. I used most of this money conducting two experiments. The first we called 'Operation Saturation'. This was a literature programme aimed at reaching every high school student in the city's trouble areas. In our literature we tackled problems such as drug addiction, promiscuity, drinking, masturbation and gang violence, offering help from the Bible. We worked hard on this programme, bringing hundreds of young people from local churches into the operation to distribute our booklets. At the end of three months, however, we could point to just a handful of boys and girls who had been truly changed as a result.

So we turned to our second experiment: television. I gathered together one hundred boys and girls who had been in trouble and found the way out. We formed an all teenage choir and every week for thirteen weeks we put on a television show. The format was simple and fresh. The kids sang, then one of the boys or girls told his story.

We were encouraged by the rating this show received: we were apparently very popular among the teen-agers of the city. But there was one trouble. Television is expensive. Kids all over the metropolitan area sent in their nickels and dimes to help support the show, but even so, at the end of our first thirteen weeks we were $4,500 in debt.

'It looks like we're going to have to cancel the series before we can really measure results,' I said to our committee, in a special meeting called to consider the crisis.

Everyone seemed to agree. We wanted to continue the experiment for another thirteen weeks, but there just didn't seem to be a way.

Suddenly a man stood up in the rear of the meeting. I had never seen him before: he wore a round collar and I thought at first he was an Episcopal priest.

'I would like to make a suggestion,' this gentleman said. He introduced himself to us: he was the Reverend Harald Bredesen, a Dutch Reformed minister from Mount Vernon, New York. 'I've seen your shows, and they have a fresh quality about them that I like. Before you decide definitely to cancel, I wonder if you'd come talk to a friend of mine.'

I agreed with a shrug, not understanding what it was all about, but knowing enough about the strange methods of the Holy Spirit to wonder if He was about to open doors for us.

The next day Harald and I went to visit Chase Walker, a magazine editor in Manhattan. Mr Walker listened attentively to the story of our work and how it got started. He seemed interested, but at the end of the conversation, he also seemed puzzled.

'Just what is it you want me to do?' he said.

'I'll be honest with you,' said Harald. 'We want $10,000.'

Mr Walker blanched. So did I.

Then Mr Walker began to laugh. 'Well, I appreciate the compliment anyhow. But I certainly don't have $10,000. And fund raising is out of my line. How did you happen to think of me in connection with this need?'

'I can't really answer that question,' said Harald. 'I've had the most remarkable feeling, ever since I learned that this programme might have to be cancelled, that somehow you held the key. Every time I'd think about it I'd think, Chase Walker! Nothing more specific than that.' Harald paused hopefully. Mr Walker said nothing. 'Well,' said Harald, disconsolately, 'I was wrong. But these hunches, when they come so strong, usually mean something.'

Mr Walker rose from his chair, bringing the interview to a close. 'I'll let you know if I get any ideas. In the meanwhile, thanks for sharing the story with me.'

We were actually out the door of his office, when suddenly Mr Walker called us back:

'Say Harald, David. Wait a moment . . .'

We turned around and went back into Walker's office. 'Something funny has just occurred to me. I got a telegram today I don't understand at all.' He fished around among the papers on his desk and came up with it. It was from W. Clement Stone, President of the Combined Insurance Company of Chicago, a friend of Walker's. 'Disregard previous telegram,' it said. 'I will be at the Savoy Hilton Wednesday.'

'That's today,' said Mr Walker. 'But I never got any previous telegram. And why should he let me know he's in town when we had no plans to get together? I wondered whether his secretary got my name confused with someone else's . . .'

Walker stared curiously at Harald for a moment, then picked up a pen and scribbled a note. 'Go up to the Savoy,' he said, handing us the note in an unsealed envelope. 'Ask for Mr Clement Stone. If he's in, you can use this as an introduction, and just see what develops. Read it if you want to.'

We did, waiting for the elevator out in the hall. 'Dear Clem,' it said. 'This is to introduce David Wilkerson who is doing a remarkable job with teen-agers in this city. David needs $10,000 for his work. You might listen to his story carefully, and, if it interests you, help him out. Chase.'

'This is the silliest thing I ever heard of,' I said to Harald. 'Do you really think we ought to visit this man?'

'Of course,' said Harald. There was no doubt at all in his mind.

Twenty minutes later we were knocking on the door of a suite in the Savoy. It was now 5:30 in the afternoon. A gentleman came to the door tying a large bow tie. He was obviously dressing for dinner.

'Mr Stone?'

The man nodded.

'Excuse us, we have a note for you from Chase Walker.'

Mr Stone stood in the doorway and read the note, then asked us in. He seemed as puzzled as we were about the situation. He said that he was due downstairs in a few moments, but that if we wanted to talk while he finished dressing, he'd be glad to listen.

Fifteen minutes later, Mr Stone was ready to leave and I had barely launched into a description of Teen-Age Evangelism.

'I have to go now,' said Mr Stone, gently. 'But if Chase Walker recommends you, that's good enough for me. I like the sound of your work. Send me your bills. I'll pay them up to ten thousand.'

Harald and I looked at each other, stunned.

'And now if you'll excuse me, please.' Mr Stone edged toward the door. 'Why don't you finish that story on tape and sent it to me? I'll pay you a visit next time I'm in New York . . . we'll work out details . . .' and he was gone.

The $10,000 went to pay our debt, and it also paid for the second thirteen weeks, and for a film, *Vulture on My Veins*, about dope addiction among teen-agers in New York. But this money purchased more than just film and television time. It brought us a new respect for this ministry. It was becoming increasingly clear to us that the hand of the Lord was in our work. As long as we really let Him lead, miracles all along the path were going to be ours to enjoy.

Chapter Fourteen

In spite of the good reports, and in spite of the good rating that our television show received, at the end of half a year of experimenting in the medium, I began to feel more and more strongly that we were missing one vital ingredient: personal contact.

So even before the second series of TV shows was over, I started going out on the streets and talking to boys and girls face to face. As soon as I did, I knew that I had touched the live, vital key to effective work with people. Jesus did not have television or the printed word to help Him. His was a face-to-face ministry. Always, the warmth of personality was involved. I knew as soon as I returned to my original technique of going out into the streets that this was the method meant for me, too.

So each morning I closed the door at my headquarters on Victory Boulevard, stepped onto the ferry and then onto the subway, and as soon as I arrived in Brooklyn I simply started talking with the boys I met. Time and again, they responded. I could watch the change taking place before my eyes as it had in St Nicholas Arena.

But the more successful my experiences on the street, the more I realized that we had to *act* on the problem of follow-up. With most of the youngsters I was satisfied if I got them established in a good local church. But with boys who were in serious trouble, or who had no home, some closer form of follow-up was needed.

One morning, just after I'd stepped off the ferryboat at the foot of Manhattan, I walked down the stairs to the subway that would take me over to Brooklyn. The subway at this point makes a great loop, and in the turn its wheels scream piercingly. This place will always have a special meaning for me. Because it was there, among the screams of the subway, that I suddenly saw my old dream take on substance.

It sprang, full-grown, to mind. The house I had dreamed of – we might call it Teen Challenge Center – would be located in the heart of the roughest part of the city. It would be head-quarters for a dozen or more full-time workers who shared my hopes for the young people around us, who saw their wonderful potential, and their tragic waste. Each worker would be a spe-cialist: one would work with boys from the gangs, another with boys who were addicted to drugs; another would work with par-ents, another with the Little People. There would be women workers: some would specialize in girl gang members, others with girls who had sexual problems, others with addiction.

There, in Teen Challenge Center, we would create an atmosphere that was so charged with this same renewing love I had watched on the streets, that to walk inside would be to know that something exciting was afoot.

And here we could bring boys and girls who needed spe-cial help. They would live in an atmosphere of discipline and affection. They would participate in our worship and in our study. They would watch Christians living together, working together; and they would be put to work themselves. It would be an induc-tion centre, where they were prepared for the life of the Spirit.

In the summer of 1960, after I'd been working full-time in the city for close to a year, I began to talk about my dream aloud. On fund-raising trips, I preached about the need. Among our churches in New York I painted the picture as I had envisioned it. But always I was met with the same question:

'Dave, this dream of yours has one flaw: it requires money.'

This was accurate, of course. We never seemed to have more than a hundred dollars in our account at any one time. It took a good hard scolding from Gwen to shake me free from the fear of launching forth just because we had no money.

Gwen came to New York just as soon as the school year was over in Pittsburgh. I found a little apartment near the office in Staten Island. 'It's not exactly the Conrad Hilton,' I said to Gwen on the long-distance line, 'but at least we'll be together. Get packed – I'm coming to get you.'

'Darling,' said Gwen, 'I don't care if we live in the street, just as long as we live there together.'

So Gwen came east. We crowded all our furniture into four rooms again, but we were extremely happy. Gwen followed very closely all the moves of the new ministry. She was particularly interested in my dream of a working family with a Center of its own.

'David,' she said one night, just after I had complained again about lack of funds, 'you ought to be ashamed. You're going at this backwards. You're trying to raise your money first, and then buy your home. If you're doing this in faith, you should commit yourself to your Center first, David, then raise your money for it.'

At first it sounded just like a woman's thinking. But the more I dwelled on the thought, the more it reminded me of biblical stories. Wasn't it always true that man had to act first, often with what seemed a foolish gesture, before God performed His mighty miracles? Moses had to stretch his arm over the sea before it parted; Joshua had to blow some horns before the walls of Jericho fell; perhaps I had to commit myself to the purchase of a new Center before the miracle could come to pass.

————————

I got together with my Central Committee, which was really just a fancy name for the group of six ministers and three laymen, all men of wonderful spiritual vision, who were interested enough in young people to give time to our organization.

I told them of the growing need for a home where gang members and narcotics addicts could associate with Christian workers. I told them about Gwen's feeling that we ought to commit ourselves to a place first, then worry about paying for it later. The committee was willing to go along with the idea. 'We can think of it as an open experiment in faith,' suggested Arthur Graves, one of the ministers on our Board.

This is the sequence of events that immediately followed our decision:

On December 15, 1960, at two o'clock in the morning while I was deep in prayer, I received the sudden clear impression that there was a particular street in Brooklyn we were supposed to investigate. We knew that our home should be close to the heart of the troubled Bedford-Stuyvesant area. So we had been making our first tentative inquiries along Fulton Street. But now came the name Clinton Avenue.

Quickly I got out a map and located the street. There it was, just a black line on a piece of paper, but I drew a line around it as if it were already settled that this was to be the future address of Teen Challenge Center.

The next day I called several of the members of the committee and we agreed to meet on Clinton Avenue to see what kind of houses, if any, might be available. Before I set out I called Paul DiLena, our treasurer, and asked how much money the organization had in the till.

'Why?' asked Paul.

'Well, we thought we'd go look at some houses on Clinton Avenue.'

'Jolly,' said Paul. 'Right now we have a balance of $125.73.'

'Ummm.'

'That doesn't bother you?'

'Not if our experiment works. We'll keep you posted.'

The very first house we looked at seemed to fit our needs. It was an older building with a decaying 'For Sale' sign out front, and although it was somewhat depressing, at least the price of $17,000 seemed reasonable. An old gentleman showed us around. We actually got to the stage of talking money with him. And the terms sounded good. We went back wondering at how swiftly all this had transpired. But when we came back the next day, the old gentleman began to stall. This went on for several days until finally we began to wonder if we were supposed to look elsewhere.

So we decided to look at another house on Clinton Avenue that had a 'For Sale' sign in a window. I had checked the till. We had less than a hundred dollars in the bank now. And this time, instead of looking at a $17,000 house, we were talking to the owner of a $34,000 property. His was a nursing home. In many ways it was ideal for the Center. It was completely furnished with beds, offices, accommodations for staff. The man came down in his price, too, while we were talking to him. I was ready to sign up, even though we did have just a hundred dollars in the bank, and even though the place did have a dank, institutional feel about it.

'Before we make any decisions,' said Dick Simmons, a young Presbyterian minister who was on our Board, 'I have the key to a house across the street. I think we ought to look at it.'

'How much is it?' I asked.

Dick hesitated. 'It's, uhh, $65,000.'

'Great,' I said. 'Every time we look at a new house the price goes up and our cash balance goes down. We were thinking about a $17,000 house when we had one hundred and twenty-five dollars. We were looking at a $34,000 house when we had a hundred. Now we're looking at a $65,000 place: we must have paid some big bills.'

The $65,000 house was a mansion. I must admit that my heart leapt when I saw it. It was a stately Georgian house built of red brick, and just as solid-looking as Monticello.

What a shock awaited us, though, when we stepped inside.

Never have I seen such a shambles. The house had been unoccupied for two years. For several years before that, students from a nearby college had used it for a combination clandestine flophouse and brothel. An old recluse lived in the place now, illegally. He was one of these old men who finds his security in accumulated junk, and he had filled every room in the house with newspapers, broken bottles, skeleton umbrellas, baby carriages and rags. Each morning he set out with a grocery trolley, collecting trash from the neighbours' garbage which he would tote back into the house and stash away. Technically he was a caretaker, I guess, but the owners had long ago ceased to expect anything of him. Most of the water pipes were broken, plaster fell from the ceilings and walls, banisters lolled on their sides and doors were ripped from their hinges.

But through it all you could quickly sense that this had once been a truly regal home. There was a private elevator going up to the second floor. There was a whole attic of servants' quarters. The basement was dry and sound, as were the walls. We walked through the sad debris, silent until all of a sudden in a loud and clear voice, almost as if he were preaching, Harald Bredesen, our Dutch Reformed pastor from Mount Vernon, said:

'This is the place. This is the place God wants for us.'

There was something so commanding about his voice that it had the quality of prophecy. The note of urgency and sureness in his voice lived with me throughout the next days, and had a lot to do, I think, with the quality of the experiments we proceeded to make.

When Dick Simmons talked with the owners, as he returned the keys, he told them frankly that a price of $65,000 might be appropriate for the house in perfect condition, but had they seen it lately? The owners came down in their price. Dick talked some more. The owners came down again. Before he got them to the point where they rather vehemently said, 'That's our rock-bottom dollar,' Dick had brought the asking price down to $42,000!

'So?' I asked Dick. 'So it's a great bargain: we still have our hundred dollars in the bank.'

Actually, I think, I wasn't too anxious to buy the property at 416 Clinton Avenue. There was so much work to do on the building that weeks of labour would be required just to make the place usable. I was anxious to move ahead with the creative work of the Center, not to spend time repairing an old building.

On the other hand, if we were intended to move into this house, who was I to object? Before I took another step I wanted to make certain that we were in God's will.

So that night, during my prayer time, I placed the question before the Lord.

'You have helped me know Your will in the past, Lord, by giving me a sign.' I thought back over the time we asked God's help in deciding whether or not to take the pastorate in Philipsburg, and whether or not to sell the television set. 'I'd like to ask permission to put one more fleece before You, Lord.'

The next day I went down to Glad Tidings and had a long talk with Mrs Marie Brown, co-pastor with Stanley Berg of the fine old church. I took up with her again our needs, our reason for wanting a Center, and I described to her the building we had found.

'David,' said Mrs Brown, 'this has every feel of being right. If you were to buy the building, when would you need the binder?'

'Within one week.'

'Would you like to come down to church Sunday afternoon and make an appeal? I know this isn't a good time, in the afternoon and just before Christmas. But you can come if you want to.'

It was a tremendous opportunity, and I was glad to say I would come. But still, I asked God for a miracle. I wanted to know for *sure* that He was in our plans. I knew that the most Glad Tidings had ever raised for home missions at a single request was $2,000. We needed more than twice that amount. The ten-per-cent binder alone would come to $4,200.

'But Lord,' I said that night in prayer, 'if *You* want us to have that building, You can let us know for sure by allowing us to raise that in a single afternoon.' That was difficult enough, but I went on, like Gideon, to make things more difficult. 'And furthermore, Lord, let me raise that amount without mentioning how much we need.' I paused. 'And furthermore,' I said, 'let me raise it without even making an appeal. Let this be something the people do out of their own hearts.'

Well, after I'd put all those fleeces before the Lord, I felt rather foolish. It was clear that I didn't really want to go into the work-filled building. But I'd made the prayer, and I waited to see what would happen.

––––––––––

Sunday afternoon arrived, the Sunday before Christmas, 1960. I preached a very simple sermon. Deliberately, I tried to make it just as coldly factual as I could. I stated our problem, and our hope, and I told the stories of a few boys we had already reached. At the end of the service, I said:

'Folks, I'm not going to make an emotional appeal. I want this to be of the Spirit if it's to be done at all. He knows how much we need. I'm going to leave, now, and go down into the basement. If it should occur to you that you want to give a certain amount to this work, I'll be glad to hear from you.'

And so, slipping out the back way, I went downstairs to the basement. I sat down behind an old pulpit there, and began to wait. I'll never forget the horror of those minutes as they slipped away. I broke out into a cold sweat, which surprised me: I had not known until that moment that I really wanted the 416 Clinton Avenue building. A minute passed, and there was no sound of steps on the stairs. Two minutes passed. Five. Ten whole minutes went by and I had given up: I was really rather glad that it was all over. At least I knew that my fleece hadn't worked.

And then the door at the end of the hall opened softly. In stepped an old, old lady. She came across the room with tears in her eyes. 'Reverend Wilkerson,' she said, 'I've been praying for fifteen years for this work to be raised up. Here's ten dollars. It's all I can give, a widow's mite; but I know it will multiply and be greatly used.' But before she left the room, the back door opened again and a fellow propped it wide with a chair; and after that a steady stream came in. The next person was a lady about fifty years old and she said:

'Reverend Wilkerson, I've been paid some money from Social Security. I want to give it to your boys.'

I was completely overwhelmed. I had never seen anything like what was happening. The next person to come up was a man; he gave us two hundred dollars. The next gave three hundred dollars. A little boy came up and said he had only fourteen cents, but he said:

'God is in this. You're getting all I got.'

Each person seemed to have a specific amount he was supposed to give. A schoolteacher, Pat Rungi, came up and said, 'David, I don't make too much money but I do work with teenagers like you do. And I know what you're up against. If you could take a postdated cheque, I'd like to donate twenty-five dollars.'

It took fifteen minutes for the line simply to walk through and lay its money on the desk. But each person brought more than just money: he brought encouragement and above all he brought a real joy to his giving so that I felt the joy too. When, finally, the last person left, I took the pile of bills and cheques up to Mrs Brown's office. And there we counted it. The amount? $4,400!

I told Mrs Brown then about the fleeces I had put before the Lord. She was as excited as I. She kept speaking about the event as a miracle and over and over again she made reference to the fact that the church had never seen anything like it. She was more convinced than ever that God was in the project.

The one thing that I did not confide to Mrs Brown was my puzzlement over that extra two hundred dollars. We'd asked for $4,200 for the binder and we'd received $4,400. I suppose it was childish of me, expecting the miracle to be so neat: but why were we given that extra two hundred dollars? Was it divine abundance, or some celestial overflow of riches? Was it a mistake in addition, or had someone written a cheque that he could not pay?

None of it proved the case. When all the reckoning was through it was quite clear that we had simply been given two hundred dollars more than we'd asked for.

Then, a few days later, sitting in my office, I was talking over the final costs of putting down our $4,200 binder with our attorney, Julius Fried.

'You have the cheque for forty-two hundred, David?'

I handed it to him with a prayer of thanks.

Julius moved uneasily in his chair as if he had something unpleasant to bring up. 'You know of course that I'm not charging the Center anything for my services ...'

It was a peculiar thing to say; Julius was on our Board and I'd always assumed his time was a gift to our project.

'But the other lawyers have got to be paid, and then there's ...'

'What are you driving at, Julius?'

'We're going to need some unexpected money, and we'll have to have the cheque at the time we put down the binder.'

'How *much* money, Julius?'

'Two hundred dollars.'

The rest of the money for the balance of the $12,000 down payment we had agreed upon came to us in an equally peculiar manner. The following Sunday, at Bethpage, Long Island, a challenged congregation came streaming forward at the close of the meeting and pressed over $3,000 into my hands. The following week, Arthur Graves called me to announce a decision his church had made:

'David,' he said, 'my Board has voted to send me to the closing with a blank cheque. You can fill it in for the amount needed to close the deal.'

And that is how it worked out that God provided us with precisely the amount we needed for the creation of Teen Challenge Center. Down to the penny, we were provided for. On the day we were handed the keys to the beautiful Georgian mansion on Clinton Avenue, I said to my wife:

'Gwen, you were right. It took a woman to show us the way. Do you realize that within just one month from the time you challenged me to step out in faith we have raised $12,200?'

Gwen was as pleased as I. 'When is the second mortgage due?' she asked.

'Not until next fall.'

It sounded so far off. I had no idea at all of the tremendous year that lay ahead of us, a year that would keep us so busy and so dizzy in amazement that the arrival of autumn, with its due date on the $15,000 second mortgage, would be upon us with devastating swiftness.

Chapter Fifteen

It's unbelievable how much junk one old man can accumulate. We discovered whole rooms we did not even know existed, because the door was covered with ceiling-high piles of debris.

'How ever are we going to get this stuff out of here?' Gwen asked one morning when she came down to look over the property with me. And then she answered her own question. 'Why don't you get some of the pastors to get up a teen-agers' work party?'

And that's just what we did. One overcast Saturday morning toward the end of January, three cars pulled up and out swarmed fifteen young boys and girls jabbering and yelling and proclaiming that they'd make short shrift of any junk we could show them. But this was while they were looking at their assignment from the outside. When they went in, and were taken from attic to basement, I could watch the enthusiasm drain out of them. Each step they had to lift a foot high to make headway. They slithered and slid over the piles of newspaper and glass until they were panting, just trying to grasp the size of the task.

But those kids did a wonderful job. They started at the front of the building and cleared a path for themselves, and room by room, floor by floor, they kept steadily at it until they had carried every bit of that junk out into the backyard.

Here, Paul DiLena took over. He had alerted the Sanitation Department of the job ahead of them.

'I think there will be at *least* four truckloads of trash to haul off,' he said.

Later Paul told me of a little drama with the foreman of the crew which, to him, said more about the spirit of our project than any previous sign: the Sanitation Department refused its tip.

Paul said the trucks arrived at 416 Clinton on schedule but that the men did not start to work. The junk piled higher and higher on the sidewalk and street and the sanitation crew just stood around. When Paul saw what was happening he caught on right away.

'All right,' he said, 'how much do you want?'

'Thirty dollars,' came the quick answer.

Paul shrugged his shoulders as one used to the ways of New York and acceded. Rather than hold the project up, he would pay the necessary gratuity himself – when the job was done.

Hours later the last of the trucks was filled. Six garbage trucks had rumbled down the street, groaning under their burden. The foreman came and asked Paul if everything was all right.

'Perfect,' said Paul. 'You did a good job. I guess you want your money now.' He started to reach for his wallet.

'What money?' said the foreman. And then he laughed, but it was a forced laugh, Paul said; the kind that tried to cover up emotion. 'Look, Mister, those kids of yours told me what you're doing here. I've got a teen-ager of my own. Do you think we'd take *money* for helping you out?'

And with that he got into his truck, revved it up and stormed away with a show of one who was really pretty tough.

———————

At the end of three weeks we were finally ready to begin work on the house itself. Painters from various churches arrived, and room by room we covered up the 'art work' with which students from the nearby college had decorated the walls. Then plumbers came: they had to tear the walls apart as new frozen and burst pipes were discovered. All this cost money, which I had to raise by taking time out for flights all over the country to make appeals. One real blow came when the city announced that before we could get a Certificate of Occupancy, a complete sprinkler system had to be installed in the building. The cost: five thousand dollars. Off I flew again, taking time out from the work I really wanted to do, just to raise money. Even so, I could never have done all the fund-raising by myself. Everyone on the Board helped in his own way. One minister, for instance, Grady Finnin, travelled around the country to present our needs. Another member of the Board was Martin Karl, a very success-ful professional singer, who used to be with the Mariners' Quartet on the Arthur Godfrey show. You can imagine the drop in income Marty took when he came to work for us as a singing ambassador. Marty took this challenge literally across the coun-try, telling about the Center that was starting in New York.

Finally, the last painter and the last plumber left the Center, and we settled back to look at what had happened before our eyes. With less than a hundred dollars in the bank, God had raised up this home. But now we had to put it to use. We wanted to fill it with His children. But before we could do that we had to give His children a place to sit down. We had a fine building, but there was nothing in it.

It was at this stage of our experience that I realized how much God wanted all sorts of people to be a part of our work. We started pretty much as an Assemblies of God programme, and before we knew it, we had an Episcopalian and a Presbyterian and a Baptist and a Dutch Reformed committee member. And we had attracted the interest of some truly influential businessmen.

One, for instance, was Mr Walter Hoving, President of Bonwit Teller and also of Tiffany's in New York. Mr and Mrs Hoving took a personal hand in introducing us to people we would never have met without their help. One afternoon, Mrs Hoving held a luncheon at the exclusive River Club to which she invited 'just a few people who should know about you'. Fifty people showed up. A converted drug addict stood up and told very simply how his life had been changed. There was not a person in that dining room who was not deeply stirred.

Walter Hoving became the President of our Board of Advisers. 'Since you're one of us now, Mr Hoving,' said Paul DiLena, 'we would like to return the courtesy of your generous meal at the River Club. Do you like lasagna?'

It was Mrs Hoving who answered. She loved lasagna, but it was so hard, she said, to get the real thing. Which is how it happened that the Hovings were invited to the home of the DiLenas for a mouth-watering meal of home-baked Italian specialties. As we all sat around Mrs DiLena's table, I couldn't help but say a private prayer of thanks that God was bringing people from so many different backgrounds into this work.

Another business friend of Teen Challenge Center was Mr Grant Simmons, Jr, President of the Simmons Bed Company. We were introduced to Mr Simmons through the Hovings, and we went to him with a specific request. We needed twenty beds. For an hour we sat in Mr Simmons' Park Avenue offices telling him about our hopes and about the strange way God was working in the city. Mr Simmons was generous not only with his time but with his substance. From that day on many a boy who is used to sleeping on subway benches has slept at the Center on Simmons beds and mattresses.

To me, one of the real functions of our ministry is getting people like Walt Hoving, Grant Simmons and Clem Stone interested in the work of Pentecostals. I would often hear remarks like this: 'I'll have to admit,' said one of our Episcopalian Board members who had been to a service at our chapel, 'that I was a little shocked when I first heard your young people "praising the Lord" and watched them raise their hands as they prayed. But I'll also have to admit that there was something very real going on in our hearts. We Episcopalians talk about the Real Presence of Christ. He's here in this home.'

This was the highest compliment our work has ever received. It is this Presence that makes the healing work of the

Teen Challenge Center possible. That sense of Presence has grown steadily, but its greatest growth took place when we began to put our dreams into action.

We planned to use the home in this way:

Eventually we would have twenty workers at the Center. Each morning these young men and women would rise, have breakfast, and then spend the morning in prayer and study. This would be an essential part of our work. I had long ago discovered that too much running around, without a base of quiet meditation, produces little of value.

After lunch, our street day would begin. Teams of two or three workers would start walking over a prescribed route, keeping an eye out for signs of trouble. They would be trained to spot the symptoms of narcotics addiction; they would be on the lookout for the teen-age alcoholic, or for the girl prostitute. They would talk to gang members, especially the members of fighting gangs.

And they would go not with an eye to gaining converts but with an eye to meeting need. The conversions would take care of themselves. If we really met a human need, the world would beat a path to our door.

Most of the teen-agers we contacted in this way would never live at the Center. We would put them in touch with a minister near their home and work through him. We would keep careful records and follow up regularly until it was clear these youngsters could stand on their own.

But some boys and girls would be sick enough to need special attention. They would be brought to the Center, the boys to live in the top-floor dormitory with the men workers on our staff; the girls to live on the second floor with the women and with the married members of our staff. We expected to be working almost exclusively with boys, but if a girl were in need we would not turn her away.

The key to this whole plan lay with the workers.

Where was I going to find twenty bright and aggressive yet empathetic and healthy young men and women, who would work for ten dollars a week (all the budget would allow)?

For this munificent sum, they would literally risk their lives. Even as I began to face the problem of finding my staff, one of our boys was knifed on the street. His name was Carlos. Carlos had been a member of one of the worst fighting gangs in New York, the Suicides. After his life had been changed, Carlos wanted to go back to his gang and tell them what had happened to him. One day he took it upon himself to do just that. As soon as he came upon members of his old gang, Carlos was surrounded.

'I hear you got religion,' said the leader of the Suicides.

'That's right,' said Carlos.

'And I hear you won't fight no more.'

'That's right,' said Carlos.

The boy pulled out his shim. 'You'll fight if I stab you,' he said.

Years of training had taught Carlos that this challenge was real. He jumped sideways and ripped off an automobile radio antenna which makes a vicious improvised weapon. Then, abruptly, Carlos changed his mind. He broke the antenna across his knee and threw it on the ground.

'No. I'm not going to fight,' he said.

And with that the leader of the Suicides stabbed Carlos. He rammed his shim hilt-deep into Carlos' ribs. The blood gushed from the wound as Carlos slumped to the sidewalk. The Suicides ran away, leaving Carlos crying for help. By the time the boy reached Cumberland Hospital it was touch-and-go whether he would live. When he was finally released it was with the doctor's friendly warning not to preach to boys who carried knives.

Carlos paid no attention to him, but went back immediately to his street preaching. Perhaps *because* of this incident he became one of our most effective workers.

But who was going to run this kind of risk? How many boys like Carlos were there?

As if in answer to this question, one morning shortly after we had brought the building into more or less usable condition, I received a wire from the Central Bible College in Springfield, Missouri, asking me to go there for a lecture. I accepted the invitation, flew out, and presented the challenge of our streets to the student body. It was a wonderful service in which everyone felt the same gentle moving of the Holy Spirit.

Afterwards, the President of the school stood up and made a rather amazing statement, saying that he thought our work was the closest thing he had seen to the challenge found in apostolic times. He offered financial help to any needy student who wanted to go to New York to work with us on the streets. Those who were interested were to meet me in the school library.

When I got to the library a few minutes later, seventy young people were standing in line!

Out of these seventy, I knew we could only use twenty workers. So I really went to work painting a dark picture. I promised them no money. They would even have to pay their own way to New York. All we could give them was a place to stay and food to eat. And I stressed that they were going to risk their lives. I told them about Carlos and two other boys who were beaten on the streets. Then I told them there would be lots of scullery work involved, doing dishes and scrubbing floors and getting the home ready.

To my surprise we eliminated only about twenty.

So I had to leave the choice to the faculty at the school. By the time I left Springfield, we had chosen sixteen young men and women to come to New York as workers. Four more were chosen from Lee College in Tennessee. One by one, a few weeks later, they began to arrive. They came carrying their suitcases and craning their necks. They were all a little frightened, I think, at the strange new sights of New York; and when I took them upstairs to their stark, barracklike dormitories, I know they were wondering what they had gotten into. Here are extracts from a letter written by one of our girls shortly after she arrived:

My dearest family:

Greetings from New York City! I arrived in the Great
City at 8:15 p.m. last night. The place was full of people,
but God helped me. T.A.E. wasn't listed in the phone
book because it's new, but I found out the number and
someone came with a car and all my friends came right
after me. I had no trouble on the way. None of my buses
were late. From Chicago to N.Y. we stopped for three
meals and two stops, so it was comfortable.

My job and plans here are as follows:

Personal evangelism among girls.

Monday – free to do as I wish.

Tuesday – Street evangelism and street services.

Wednesday – Hospital visitations to teen-age girls.

Thursday – Jail visits to girls.

Friday – Street evangelism and street services.

Saturday – Work with denominational churches.

Sunday – Work with Pentecostal churches.

In charge of girls as dorm counsellor. See that the rooms
are clean and homework done, etc.

In charge as music director.

We are praying for a person to pioneer the girl evangelism
with me.

There were three murders in Joe's section this week.
I must go help cook supper. Don't forget to go
to church. I love you.

I'll never forget the evening when I was finally able to say to Gwen, 'Well, honey, we're open for business.'

We were standing in the little chapel of the Center. This room had at one time been the formal drawing room of the old house, and there was a large fireplace against one wall. A richly carved mantel stuck out into the room, and as I talked to Gwen I leaned up against this mantel.

I reminded her of the evening, just a year and a half earlier, when I'd stood in the moonlit church yard in Philipsburg, watching the wheat wave in the breeze. Now the Lord had brought us to the harvest field. He had given us the tools: twenty fine workers and a belief in the power of the Holy Spirit to change lives.

'Darling,' said Gwen, 'look!'

I stood forward and tried to make out what she was pointing to on the mantelpiece. And then I saw, too. There, beautifully carved into the fireplace in our chapel, was the bas-relief of a sheaf of wheat, brought in, tied and harvested.

Chapter Sixteen

As soon as we got our workers settled I took them into the chapel and, standing before the bas-relief of the harvested wheat, I gave them a briefing on the make-up of a New York fighting gang.

'"Violence" is the key word to remember about these gangs,' I told the young workers. 'It can express itself directly by a war in which boys get killed, or by rape or street murder or muggings. Or it can express itself indirectly by sadism and homosexuality, lesbianism, promiscuity, narcotics addiction, drunkenness. These ugly things are the rule, not the exception, among the jitterbugging gangs in New York.'

It was important, I thought, for our young workers to know the reason for this pathetic state. 'We preachers are likely to use words a little too glibly,' I said, 'but some of our professional vocabulary is wonderfully descriptive if you think about its real meaning. For instance, we speak of *lost* sinners. As I got to know these gang members, I couldn't escape the feeling that they were literally acting as if they were lost. They wandered around scared and they looked furtively over their shoulders. They carried weapons against unknown dangers, ready at a moment's notice to run or to fight for their lives. These lost boys group together for protection, and there you have the making of a gang.'

There was one all-important fact that came out of my work with street boys. Virtually without exception they had no real home. Their slang words for home were 'prison' and 'horror house'. I wanted our workers to know this situation from personal experience, so I took a few of them into the home of one of the street boys I knew.

When we arrived, the door was open; no one was at home.

'You can see why they call it a horror house,' whispered a young girl worker from a Missouri farm. And it was true. A family of five lived in this single room. There was no running water, no refrigeration, no stove except for the single-burner hot plate with its frayed wire that sat on a chest of drawers. There was no toilet: down the hall in a single, stinking stall was a toilet and a faucet which served eight families on the floor. The ventilation in the apartment was poor, and a strong odour of gas hung permanently in the air. The room's one window looked out onto a blank brick wall, eight inches away. For light the family had the use of a single forty-watt bulb which hung naked from the centre of the ceiling.

'And do you know what these people have to pay for their horror house?' I asked. 'Twenty dollars a week: eighty-seven a month. I figured it up once: the landlord here makes just over $900 every month on this single tenement, and that is almost all profit. It isn't uncommon for a slum landlord to get a twenty per cent net return on his investment each year.'

'Why doesn't the family just move?'

'Because a Negro or a Puerto Rican cannot really live where he chooses,' I had to admit. 'This is a town of ghettos.'

'Can't they get into one of the housing projects?'

To answer this question we got in the car and drove a mile away to a great complex of apartments. These projects, many people thought, were the answer to New York's slums. Bulldozers moved into an overcrowded area, like the one we had just visited; they tore down the old tenements and built towering light new buildings in their place. In theory, you housed in these apartments the old tenants, and also the old corner grocer and neighborhood lawyer and family doctor. Actually, it did not work out this way. The old tenant, and the storeowner, and one professional man couldn't wait two years for the new building to be finished, so they moved away. Then when the project was completed, who was shoved to the top of the priority list? The most desperate people, of course: the relief cases.

The result was twofold. First, there was a completely uprooted neighbourhood. Everybody in it was *lost*. None of the old institutions were left, none of the older and more stable population of professional men and businessmen. Second, because relief cases had priority, the projects in effect created mammoth eddies in the city into which floated all the people of New York who, for one tragic reason or another, could not take care of themselves.

The project we visited was not more than a few years old, but already serious signs of disintegration were evident. We walked past desolate lawns that had long ago been abandoned. Several of the windows on the ground floor were broken and unrepaired. There was obscene writing on the walls. The halls smelled of urine and cheap wine.

Here, too, we visited a family I knew. The mother had been drinking. None of the beds in her home had been made; dishes from several meals lay on the kitchen table. The boy we had come to visit sat on a torn hassock staring, never speaking, apparently not even aware that we were there.

'I've known that boy in other moods,' I said, once we were outside again. 'He can be just as overactive as he is overquiet now. Usually he's out on the streets. Thrown out. He can only come home when his mother has passed out, drunk.'

And this, I pointed out again, was the making of a teenage fighting gang. Lump a thousand tortured families together in a single neighbourhood and you have a floating population of teen-agers who are hostile and afraid, who flock together looking for security and a sense of belonging. They will create a home for themselves by fighting for a 'turf' which is theirs, and which no stranger can violate. This is their fortress.

It is marked out with military precision. The northern boundary is the firehouse, the southern boundary the superhighway, the western the river, and the eastern Flannigan's candy store.

There isn't much these boys can do with their time. Many of them are degradingly poor. I met one fourteen-year-old who had not eaten a real meal in two days. His grandmother, who took care of him, gave him twenty-five cents each morning and chased him out of the house. For breakfast he had a seven cent Coke, for lunch a fifteen-cent hot dog from a street vendor, and for supper he laughed and said he was going on a diet. All evening he nibbled on penny candy.

Strangely, though, although the boys I've met never seem to have enough money for food, they always have enough for a bottle of wine.

'It really frightens me to see how much drinking these young people do,' I said to our workers. 'Many of the street boys drink wine all day long.' They are seldom really drunk – they can't afford it – nor are they quite sober. They start drinking just as soon as they meet, at ten or eleven in the morning, and continue until funds run out.'

Occasionally from somewhere, usually from a purse-snatching or from extorting lunch-money from younger children, enough money comes into the common till to afford stronger stuff, and on more than one such occasion in our neighbourhood this has led to tragedy.

When we got back to the Center, I took our workers into the chapel again and told them the story of Martin Ilensky. Martin was a high school senior who worked part-time to help support his invalid mother. One day when he was not working he went to a vodka party at the 'horror house' of another high school boy. Ten teen-agers were there, six boys and four girls. After an hour of drinking vodka and dancing to rock 'n' roll, the vodka ran out. The boys took a collection for beer, but Martin refused. A fight followed. A twelve-inch German sword appeared from one of the boys' waistbands. There was a swift jab and Martin Ilensky lay dead on the kitchen floor.

'Now then . . .' I knew the words I was about to say would bother some of our workers, fresh from the seminary as they were. I leaned back with my hands locked behind my head. 'Suppose you could have talked to Martin Ilensky on some street corner for a few minutes. Remember: it is his fate to die if he goes to that party. What would your first words to him be?'

'I'd tell him that Jesus saves,' piped up one boy.

'That's what I was afraid.'

Young eyes looked up puzzled.

'We've got to be very careful,' I said, 'that we don't become parrots. I try to keep my ear tuned for phrases – religious terms – that I've heard before. Then when I'm on the street I never use such a phrase without first saying a prayer that I can give it all the power it had when it was spoken for the very first time.

'What,' I said, 'do you really mean when you say "Jesus saves"?'

Of course these boys and girls knew the answer to that – they weren't just mouthing often-heard answers now; they were talking about something that had happened to them.

'Well, it means,' said the girl, 'that you're born again.'

Still, the words had a pat sound to them. They didn't have that ring of freshness we had to capture if we were going to touch Martin Ilensky before he was stabbed with a twelve-inch German sword.

'What happened to you when you were born again?' I asked this girl. And as soon as I did the young lady grew quiet. She hesitated a moment before she answered. In a voice that caught the attention of the entire room she told about a change that had come into her life one day. She talked of how she had been lonesome, and afraid, and of how her life didn't seem to be going anywhere.

'I'd heard about Christ,' she said, 'but the name was just a word. Then one day a friend told me that Christ could take away my lonesomeness and my fear. We went to church together. The preacher invited me to come forward, and I did. I knelt down in front of everybody and asked this "Christ", who had just been a name, to work a change in my life. And nothing has been the same since then,' she said. 'I really am a new person, which is why they say you're "born again", I suppose.'

'You lost your lonesomeness?'

'Yes. Altogether.'

'What about your fear?'

'That too.'

'And Christ is more to you now than just an empty word?'

'Of course. A word can't change things.'

The room was silent. 'Nor could empty *words* have changed things for Martin,' I said. 'Keep this boy in mind when you go out onto the street tomorrow.'

———————

By late Spring, 1961, Teen Challenge Center was in full operation. Every day – even on Mondays when they were supposed to be off – our young workers were out on the streets of Brooklyn and Harlem and the Bronx, looking for teen-agers who needed them. They went to hospitals and jails, to schools and courts. They held street meetings in Greenwich Village and in Coney Island and in Central Park. And as they worked, the flow of young kids coming through our Center grew from a trickle to a flood. During the first month of operation, more than five hundred boys and girls had been saved, if I can give that word its fullest meaning. Five hundred boys and girls had been gripped by the message of the Spirit; their lives had been radically changed; they left the gangs; they sought jobs; they started going to church.

Of this five hundred, perhaps a hundred came to the Center for special counselling. And of this hundred, only a handful were in such trouble that they needed to live at the Center, absorbing directly its atmosphere of love.

One of the first boys to experience a healing of personality at our Center was George. George was a handsome boy of nineteen – too handsome, in fact, for his own good. George had no home. He had been kicked out of his natural home by parents who were disgusted by his behaviour with older women: the young boy was constantly getting himself involved with women twice his age. His methods were always the same. He would strike up an acquaintance with a lonesome older woman. He would intrigue her with a tale of the hard life he led, gain her sympathy and ask to see her again, 'just to talk. It does me so much good.'

These conversations usually turned into deeper involvements, and soon George had a new friend. He would move into her apartment, where the woman would treat him like a son. George was a jeweller by trade. As soon as he made his way into the woman's house, he managed to bring up the subject of jewellery and offered to repair her gems for her. George would leave the house with the jewels, supposedly taking them to a friend's shop, but actually heading for the nearest receiver of stolen goods.

It was a pretty shoddy life for a virile, healthy young man. But one day all that changed. George stumbled onto one of our street meetings. Although he would not talk with our workers at the time, a few days later he appeared at the Center. He came in 'just for kicks'. He felt a strange sensation of warmth the minute he walked through the doors. One of our workers, Howard Culver, saw him and struck up a conversation. Before the morning was over, George decided he wanted to start a new life. He prayed for a change to happen to him, and in that miracle we never get accustomed to, precisely that did happen.

'It was just like a great burden was suddenly lifted off my back,' George told me later. He was excited about the change that had happened to him. He couldn't stop talking about it; he kept turning it over and around to examine it in every detail.

As the days passed, George began to feel the need to repay all the money he had stolen. He got a job: a good one, for George is quite a capable young man. Every penny above what it costs him to live goes toward these debts. When they are all paid, George wants to go into the ministry.

———————

As the summer wore on and more and more boys passed through the Center, we began to face a moral problem. At one time or another, all of our boys have broken the law. What should they do about that?

It is not a simple question to answer. It would be relatively easy for a boy who had really become strong in his new life to take his punishment in jail. But to become strong usually takes time. There are many crises to pass, many dry periods to ride out, much to learn about the art of being a Christian. If a boy confesses to the police too early and is put in jail, isn't there the risk of losing him? On the other hand, he has offended society's law and it will also hold him back spiritually if he harbours guilt.

I have come to feel that there is no answer that will cover all cases. Often I am puzzled as to what recommendation to make. Pedro, for example, had been living in the Center for several days when he came to me complaining:

'I can't eat. I can't sleep. I can't sleep at all.'

'Why, Pedro?'

'I feel the weight of all my crimes. It sits on my shoulders, and I have to go to the police and confess.'

I listened to him for a while and came to the conclusion that he really did have to confess to the police ... sometime. Pedro didn't detail his crimes for me because he had too much trouble with English and I could speak very little Spanish. But he was agitated and confused and it did seem that a police confession would be the right thing. The only problem was one of timing. Pedro was so new to his changed life that a jail sentence would almost surely set him back. I recommended to Pedro that he consider waiting.

But he would have none of it.

So, to act as an interpreter, I contacted my old friend, Vincente Ortez. Together we took Pedro down to the police. The sergeant was sitting behind his desk eating a sandwich when we came in. He looked up and said, 'Yes, sir?'

'I'm Reverend Wilkerson, Director of Teen-Age Evangelism,' I said. 'I have a young boy here who was a member of the Dragon gang and he has some things he wants to confess.'

The sergeant looked at me stonily and asked me to repeat that. When I did, he put down his pencil and called me to his side and said, 'Reverend, is he a crackpot?'

'Not at all,' I said.

'We have people coming in all the time to confess things they never did. But if you think the boy's in his right mind, take him upstairs to the detectives' room.'

So we went upstairs and waited. Pedro seemed composed. Soon a detective came in and asked me right away if I had forced Pedro to come.

'No,' I said. 'He's here of his own accord.'

'You realize he might go to jail.'

I asked Vincente Ortez to explain this to Pedro in Spanish. The boy nodded his head. Yes, he understood.

So the detective got out some yellow paper and licked his pencil and settled back. He was very kind and he was very much impressed. 'All right, Pedro. Suppose you tell us what you want to confess.'

'Well,' said Pedro, through Vincente Ortez, 'do you remember that stabbing . . .?' and he proceeded to describe a knifing that had taken place in Central Park two months earlier. The detective put his pencil down and called in another officer. They remembered the incident, and their interest picked up considerably. Pedro detailed the events that led up to the knifing. He was on drugs and he needed a fix. He was with two other boys. They spotted a young man sitting by himself on a bench, circled him, robbed him and then put a knife in his stomach.

Pedro then went on to confess two robberies. The detectives kept him there from six o'clock until twelve o'clock, checking and rechecking facts. They found the boy who had been stabbed, but he had a record at the station, too, and wouldn't press charges: he didn't want to get involved. The store which Pedro had robbed twice also refused to press charges. 'I know that place,' said Vincente Ortez. 'I think they're making book on the side; they probably don't want to get involved.'

So in the end the police couldn't find anyone to press charges. They were willing to release Pedro in our custody. We went back to the Center, and the next morning, Pedro was up before anyone. He woke the entire house with his singing. He sang at the top of his lungs, and he greeted everyone with such cheeriness that we couldn't complain. Pedro was a different boy. His heart was filled with a truly amazing joy.

Not all of our boys have stories as dramatic as this. In fact, most of the young men who come to the Center and find an emotional home here are just plain lonesome kids. Their lives never amounted to a thing. They missed any sense of welcome in their natural homes because, in fact, they weren't welcome. They got into trouble but it was the petty kind of trouble that was mostly just a symptom. We have a wonderful boy, for instance, who really counts the Center as his home. He is a simple young man named Lucky.

Lucky has had a great deal of trouble coming to grips with life. He has a great smile, and a twinkle in his eye, and a warm handshake, but so often in the past, he has had difficulty getting down on the job at hand. When Lucky was eleven years old he started cutting classes and running wild all over the Bronx with a gang called the Crowns. His favourite sport was to smash the window of a patrol car and then run. He would dash across rooftops making the cops puff after him, taking daring leaps and only laughing if he missed and had to grab for life itself to the nearest fire escape.

Lucky started running with another gang, the Dragons, and at the age of fifteen he was elected their president. His term of office was rather short, because one day Lucky found himself in jail for beating up his high school home-room teacher. Six months later he was released, but still he was unable to find roots. He attended bakers' school but was incompatible with the teacher. He attended cooks' school but was incompatible with the teacher. He attended butchers' school and this time when he got into still another argument with his teacher he was told he had to leave school.

Teen Challenge Center is the only place on earth where Lucky has stayed overnight of his own free will. The moment he walked in our doors he felt as if he was coming home. 'The thing I like specially,' he says to newcomers, whom he greets with his broad smile, 'is here they don't care what your race is or what your nationality is. Look here, they've got white boys and coloured boys and Spanish boys and they're all mixed up in God.'

Lucky has had an amazingly deep religious experience. He associates the new warmth and outgoingness with the Center so strongly in fact that we're having trouble getting him to move on into the next step of his career. He doesn't want to do anything but stay right here and help us. So . . . we let him stay. Lucky is our maintenance man, and a dependable one too. He earns his ten dollars a week many times over. Some day, when he is ready, Lucky will move on, as all of our boys do.

But until that time comes, he is welcome here.

Chapter Seventeen

As the thermometer on our back porch mounted higher and higher with the summer heat, life at the Center settled into something resembling a routine. Our twenty workers were busy from early morning until late at night. This was the schedule for the day:

Rising bell at 7:00

Breakfast at 7:30

Dishes and clean-up

Personal devotions until 9:30

Group chapel from 9:30 to 11:30

Dinner at 12:00

Dishes

Prayer

Street work from 2:00 until 6:00 when we eat sack suppers together on the street.

More street work until 7:30

Back to the Center for evening services until midnight

Bed

The job of running the Center very quickly became too big for any one man, and over the months we built up a cadre of experts in specialized fields who ran the Center far better than I could have done on my own. Howard Culver, for instance, became our administrator. He saw to it that discipline was maintained; this was not always an easy task with twenty lively young collegians and an ever-changing number of young gang members on his hands. Howard's wife Barbara was a godsend: she is a registered nurse. We found her presence invaluable with undernourished youngsters, and especially with narcotics addicts whose bodies go through hell during withdrawal.

If I have a special place in my heart for the next member of our staff, I think it is understandable.

He is Nicky. What a day it was for me when Nicky walked shyly through the front door of the Center with a beautiful girl on his arm!

'Davie,' said Nicky quietly, 'I want you to meet my wife, Gloria.'

Nicky and Gloria had met on the West Coast while they were both in Bible school. I rushed forward to greet them, wringing Nicky's hand and slapping him on the back, and welcoming Gloria so warmly I'm afraid she was a little startled.

Nicky, Gloria and I sat in the office and reminisced. I found it difficult to believe this was the same boy who had threatened to kill me just three years earlier. On our first encounter Nicky had impressed me as a hopeless case. Yet here he was, sitting before me a new person – a licensed minister, bursting with plans for the future.

'What I want, Davie,' he said, leaning forward eagerly, 'is to work not just with kids, but with the parents. What's the good helping a boy if he's got to go home to a miserable family situation?'

It made sense, exciting sense. And Gloria's idea was just as sound. She wanted to work at the Center too. She loved children and her special field would be the Little People. Nicky had told her about the eight-, nine-, and ten-year-olds who run on the periphery of the gangs, and Gloria now pointed out that to reach these little ones *before* they got into serious trouble was even better than trying to pull them out of trouble later.

Our permanent staff really excited me as it grew. We were coming at the problems of the street kids from all angles. I was working with boys. Nicky with the parents. Gloria with the Little People. But there was one large gap: we had no one whose special interest was in the Debs.

Who is a Deb? And what is her relationship to the gangs?

In recent years the role of the young teen-age girl has been growing in importance in the complex make-up of the gangs. She is known as a 'Deb'. She groups together with other youngsters like herself to form auxiliaries to the boy-gangs. Often these girl-gangs take names that echo the names of their male counterpart, as in the Cobras and the Cobrettes.

The girls, I quickly discovered, were often the cause of trouble on the streets. I know of one rumble that started because a Deb from one gang complained that a boy from a rival gang made a pass at her. Later the girl confessed that she was lying all the time; she made up the story just so there would be a fight. She did it for kicks.

It is a rare thing for a Deb to be a virgin. 'Marriage is out of style, Preacher,' these girls told me, laughing. There wasn't any use my talking to them: they brazenly handled their nervousness by propositioning me. What we needed was a girl on the staff who was attractive enough to gain the Debs' respect and yet who was solid enough in her own faith not to be shaken by their taunting and laughter.

And we finally found her.

'We've got just the right girl to work with the Debs, honey,' I reported to Gwen one evening.

'Wonderful,' said Gwen. 'I hope she's pretty. She's got to be pretty for the job. I never thought I'd be urging my husband to find a pretty girl to work with.'

'She *is* pretty,' I said. 'Her name is Linda Meisner. She comes from a farm in Iowa. I just hope these city girls don't frighten her.'

Linda's job with the Debs was not an easy one. She got her introduction to the girls on her very first Saturday night at the Center. In the late afternoon, five girls walked through the door and demanded to be shown around. Linda would have been willing to oblige, but I could smell alcohol on the girls' breath and tried to postpone the visit.

'We have a service here at 7:30 that's open to the public,' I said. 'Come then; you'll be welcome.' The girls came back at 7:30, bringing a group of boys with them.

'What are we going to do, David?' Linda asked. 'The girls are quite drunk.'

'Let's start by separating them,' I said. 'Boys on one side, girls on the other.'

It did very little good. The girls giggled, mocked, blew loud bubbles on their gum, got up, and walked in and out. I saw several of the girls get out knives and start cutting their shoe strings. In the middle of my sermon, they began to argue with me from the floor of the little chapel. I turned the meeting over to an all-girl trio (which included Linda) but they couldn't sing above the noise.

Finally we just gave up trying to hold an orderly meeting and turned our attention instead to individual boys and girls. Most of the girls got out of their seats and stormed out the door, slamming it loudly not once but twice behind them. One girl who stayed went over to the fellows and put her arm around their shoulders.

'Don't believe a word of it,' she said to them, one after another.

That night the girls won. The evening broke up early with no results that we could see. This was Linda's introduction to her future friends. To cap the climax, we later learned that the same night, over on South Second, there had been a murder.

'It's hopeless, David,' said Linda the next morning. 'I don't see how I can ever work with kids as hard as these.'

'Wait till you see what the Holy Spirit can do, Linda, before you make up your mind.'

The very next Tuesday, Linda had her first experience of watching the change. Afterwards, she showed me the letter she had written to her parents:

> ... *every* minute is full of excitement and a new adventure. On Tuesday the entire gang of boys and girls returned. We wanted to have them come on different nights, but the girls begged to come in with the boys for a service. They promised not to laugh and to be good; so we let them all in. During the service, we sang 'Jesus Breaks Every Fetter'. Dave asked if there was anything that anyone would like for God to break in their lives. A fourteen-year-old girl said she would like to be delivered from heavy drinking every night. One of the girls pulled up her sleeve and asked if God could forgive this – a line showing heroin inserts. The girls behaved as well as I've seen girls behave anywhere.

From that moment on, girls from the gangs sought Linda out for help. Elaine, for instance, one of the girls from the local gang, came to Linda with a very common problem for a Deb; she said she was poisoning her life with hate. I knew Elaine. She was a hard girl; you could just feel the hatred that clung about her. She was a discipline problem at school and at home. If she was told to sit, she'd stand; if to stand, she'd sit. If she was told she had to stay in, she'd slip out; or if she was told to get out of the house, nothing could make her leave her room. Elaine's parents gave up and somehow managed to talk various relatives into boarding the girl for a part of each year.

One afternoon Elaine came to see Linda. Linda reported to me later that they sat out in the kitchen and sipped pop and talked. Elaine's first words were that she had been drinking heavily. Then she told Linda that she had recently started going to wild parties; they started off wild and grew wilder. She said that some time ago she had lost her virginity and that sex was now just a dull routine.

Suddenly, with no warning, Elaine began to cry. 'Linda,' Elaine said at last, looking up, 'do you know I never did really fool myself? I never did, once, lie down on a bed with a fellow without I knew, here,' she felt her heart, 'that it was wrong. Linda, I don't want to hate myself any more. Can you help me?'

Soon Elaine was coming regularly to our Gang Church meetings that we held every Wednesday night. She consented to stand up and tell what happened to her hate. Her face was open and fresh and free as Linda's. She was always singing or laughing. She started bringing her cousins and her friends. She stopped her drinking and her wild partying.

'Do you know why she stopped, Dave?' Linda told me. 'She just said she couldn't be bothered. She had more interesting things to do.'

And Elaine was no isolated case. Day in and day out we could count on reaching girls like Elaine with this special kind of love. I'll never forget the day Elaine put her finger on the quality of the love that redeems.

'I've finally got it figured out, Reverend Wilkerson,' said the girl. 'Christ's love is a love with no strings attached.'

Elaine is right. Christ's love is a love without angles: a love that asks nothing in return. It is a love that wants only the *best* for these boys and girls. And this is the quality that redeems.

––––––––––

In one of her letters home, Linda wrote that her life was in constant danger.

This was not an exaggeration. We do what we can to protect our workers. For instance, we have a rule that street work must be done in teams of two or three. We have a rule that girls are not allowed to make contact with boys on the street, and vice versa. And we have a rule that workers must make contact with each other at regular intervals, especially when they are working at night.

The fact remains, however, that our young students are walking into areas where armed officers of the law travel in pairs for protection. A large percentage of the teen-agers in the rougher sections of the city carry concealed weapons. If a boy is high on heroin he might easily lash out with his knife, just for kicks. But a much more serious problem is the jealousy that is aroused when our workers threaten to break up relationships.

One night Linda and a partner, Kay Ware, were out later than usual. It was near midnight on a sweltering summer night. Evening services were over and the girls should have gone to bed, but such was their interest in sharing what they had found that they headed out into the night, praying that the Holy Spirit would lead them to girls in need.

The girls came to a candy store and, looking inside, they saw four teen-agers – girls – listening to rock 'n' roll and sipping Cokes. Linda and Kay walked in and struck up a conversation with the girls. In one of those amazingly quick transitions that we had by now grown accustomed to, the four girls argued for only a few moments, then one of them began to cry.

'Come on,' said another of the foursome. 'Let's go out on the street. I don't want this jerk,' she thumbed toward the store proprietor, 'to hear this.'

So all the girls stepped outside into the sticky, sultry night. Hardly had they started talking again when all *four* of the girls started to cry like babies.

Two fellows walked up.

'What's going on?' they asked.

The teen-age girls told them to flake off. They didn't want to talk to the boys.

This aroused the boys' curiosity even more than the tears, and they pressed in. 'What are you trying to do?' they asked Linda. 'Take our girls away from us?'

One of the boys switched the approach and began to pinch Linda. 'Come over into the park, pretty one, and I'll show you something.' The other fellow joined in, then, and the two of them issued a string of suggestions to Linda and Kay that left them embarrassed and confused. But they had a good defence.

Swinging around suddenly and looking the leader of the two boys squarely in the eye, Linda said slowly, 'God bless you.'

The boy's jaw dropped. Linda turned then and picked up her conversations with the four girls and the boys sputtered a while, then one of them said:

'Hell! Let's get out of this creep's way.'

Linda and Kay went back to their talks with the teen-age girls. After a while, though, they were aware that a whole crowd of boys was descending slowly on them from many different directions.

'You better watch out,' whispered one of the teen-age girls.

Linda and Kay moved closer together, but they continued talking calmly. Then, suddenly, there was a loud laugh and a cry. All of the girls were surrounded by yelping, shouting teen-age boys. The fellows crowded in and separated Linda and Kay from the other girls.

'Say, little one, you make me mad,' said the leader of the boys. 'You talking religion to our girls? You'll take them away from us.'

And again the sex talk began. Linda and Kay heard language they'd never heard before. The boys pushed and taunted them.

From nowhere something glistened in the dark. Linda looked. One of the boys held a crescent-shaped knife in his hand that shone in the night like the moon.

Without warning he lunged at Linda. Linda slipped her body sideways. The knife slashed through her clothing. It ripped out a chunk of her dress but it did not touch her body.

Linda turned to the boy while he was still off balance. Once again she spoke the words that had helped her before. Her voice was low, and she put all the meaning she could into her words.

'God bless you.'

Then she took Kay by the arm. 'Come over to the Center tomorrow: 416 Clinton Avenue,' she said. 'We'll be expecting you.' Then she and Kay sauntered off across the street.

At first the boys followed them singing their sex calls. Then, for reasons that Linda and Kay still do not understand, the leader shouted for the boys to stop.

'Come on,' he said. 'Let's forget it. I don't feel like fooling with them.'

Linda and Kay came back to the Center shaking. But the next day they did pick up conversations with the four girls, and the next night they were out on the street again.

'I'm glad your foot is better, Larry,' Linda wrote in a causal letter home. 'I wish I could tell you what's on my heart. You can actually feel the presence of evil. I know that my life is in danger. I have only one desire . . . to burn out for God.'

Chapter Eighteen

The thing that constantly amazed me about our workers was that they could have this desire 'to burn out for God,' without themselves becoming taut, intense personalities.

I've wondered about the reason for this. And I think it's that the Center has turned out to be just what we hoped it would be: a home. Full of love, subject to a spiritual discipline, heading toward the same common goal, but free.

There's a release in that kind of atmosphere that can't be overestimated. It keeps us from becoming tied up in knots. It allows us to laugh.

I'm glad about that. It doesn't seem likely to me that any true house of God is going to be a drab and sombre place. Certainly the Center is no place for the long-of-face. If it isn't a pillow fight in the girls' dorm, or a short sheet in the boys', then it's sugar in the salt shaker. All the old wheezes.

Of course, I have to frown about this, but no one seems to pay too much attention to me. When I come chasing up the stairs bellowing like a Director that the Lights are Supposed to be Out! there is angelic snoring which lasts just long enough for me to get back downstairs. I would worry about this lack of respect for authority except that discipline really takes care of itself: we keep our young people so busy that there isn't much energy left for roughhousing. After a few minutes the fun wears thin, and the snoring becomes real.

Unfortunately for decorum, all the horseplay isn't confined to the college kids and teen-agers. Shortly after Nicky and Gloria arrived, we began what we called Operation Ganglift. Glad Tidings church has a retreat centre in upstate New York, a farm called Hidden Valley. During the hottest weeks of summer we asked permission to take a few of the boys from the gangs up to Hidden Valley for a breath of real air. Nicky and his wife came along. Lucky came too. So did a dozen other boys from the Center.

One Friday night, Nicky and Gloria decided to go for an evening stroll before retiring. Lucky and some of the boys called me aside and asked if I'd take part in a practical joke.

'You know Nicky's never been in the country,' said Lucky, who was an old hand, having been in the country once before. 'Will you take one of these candles and come along on a joke?'

'What are you going to do?'

'Nothing that'll hurt anyone. We're just going bear hunting.'

So we took candles, lit them, and started down the same path Nicky and Gloria had taken. Pretty soon we came upon the couple on their way back to the farmhouse.

'What are you doing?' asked Nicky.

'We're hunting,' said Lucky. 'We're looking for bears. Want to see their tracks?'

Lucky knelt down on the path and held his candle close to the ground. There, in the soft earth, were a series of old cow tracks. Nicky looked close, and sure enough he saw the mysterious, unknown markings in the ground. You could just see the hackles rise on his back. He drew his wife a little closer and asked for a candle.

Suddenly Lucky stood up. 'What's that?' he said. His voice was very low and frightened. He pointed up the path to an object which we could just make out in the moonlight. Sure enough, it looked for all the world like a bear, hunched over in the dark. If I hadn't known it was an old abandoned school bell silhouetted in the eerie light, I'd have been afraid myself.

This time, when we looked for Nicky, he was crouched beside his wife behind a sycamore tree. The other boys picked up stones and threw them at the bear, calling on Nicky not to be chicken and to come help them.

And then, suddenly, Nicky gave us all a laugh. He stepped out from behind his sycamore tree with his wife on his arm.

'Phooey!' he said loud and clear. 'I've got faith. I'm going to trust God. I'm trusting Him to help me *run!*'

And with that Nicky and his wife headed back to the farmhouse leaving us overcome with laughter. When we returned we all got busy and made hot chocolate for Nicky and his wife. It took six cups to get the scare out of them.

It surprised me, that summer, to discover how much of the free give-and-take we encountered at 416 Clinton Avenue centred on the kitchen.

I think maybe God saw to it, during those first long months of our work at the Center, that we never found a cook. We tried every system under the sun to keep ourselves fed, but the one that never worked out was to have a full-time cook usurp the pantry. A kitchen is always the heart of a home anyhow, and a real cook has a way of chasing you out so that she can get her work done. Thus you are chased from the heart of the home.

Not so with the Center, because we could never come up with a cook.

The result was a wonderful, chaotic, happy mess. And to understand it you must first understand where the food itself comes from. Like everything else at the Center, we get our food by praying for it. This is one of the projects in which our living-in gang members take a most active role. Each day we pray for food, and the way it comes in is a vivid lesson to boys just learning about faith. People send in a ham, potato chips, fruit, vegetables. Or they send in money not earmarked for a special purpose.

One day, however, the kids awoke and washed and went down to breakfast and there wasn't anything on the table. By the time I arrived in the office from home, the Center was buzzing with the problem of no food.

'Your prayers didn't work I guess this time, did they, Dave?' said one of the gang boys.

'Lord,' I said to myself, 'teach us a lesson in faith that will live with us forever.' And aloud, I said, 'Let's make an experiment. Here we are without food for the day, right?'

The boy nodded his head.

'And the Bible says, "Give us this day our daily bread," right?'

'If you say so.' I laughed and glanced at Reverend Culver, who shrugged and nodded his head as if to say he'd teach the boy the Lord's Prayer.

'So why don't we all go into the chapel right now and pray that we either get the food for this day or money to buy the food.'

'Before lunch, Dave?' said the boy. 'I'm getting hungry.'

'Before lunch. How many people do we have here?' I glanced around. The number in the Center was constantly shifting. On that day we could count twenty-five people who would need to be fed. I figured it would cost between thirty and thirty-five dollars to feed that number of people dinner and supper. Others agreed. So we went into the chapel, closed the door, and we all began to pray.

'While you're at it, Lord,' said the little gang boy, 'would You please see to it that we don't go hungry for the rest of the summer?'

I looked over, mildly annoyed. It seemed to me that this was stretching things a bit. But I had to admit that it would leave us freer to work at other kinds of prayer if we didn't have to pay so much attention to such basic needs as food.

One of the things about our prayer at the Center is that it tends to be a bit loud. We do pray aloud often, and there is a wonderful freedom in the Spirit that sometimes frightens people who hear it for the first time. They may think it is uncouth, without realizing that we are just expressing our true

CHAPTER EIGHTEEN **173**

feelings before God. If we feel concerned, we say so not only with our lips but with the tone of our prayer.

And this morning we were quite concerned. While we were saying so in tones that left no doubt about how we felt, a stranger walked in.

We didn't even hear when she knocked on the door of the chapel. When finally she opened the door and saw all twenty-five of us on our knees, thanking God for the food He had given us in the past and thanking Him too for the food He would be giving us, somehow, in this emergency, I'm sure she was sorry she had come.

'Excuse me,' she said, softly.

'Excuse me!' she said, louder.

I was near her and I heard and immediately got up. The rest of the workers and gang members kept right on with their prayer.

This lady was a little hesitant about coming to the point of her visit. She kept asking questions, but I noticed that the more she found out about what we were doing, the more enthusiastic she became. Finally, she asked about the prayer session. I told her about walking in that morning to discover that we had no food in the house, and about the purpose of the prayer.

'When did you begin this prayer?' the lady asked.

I figured up. 'About an hour ago.'

'Well,' she said, 'that is truly extraordinary. I knew very little about your work. But an hour ago I received a sudden impulse to do something that is completely out of character for me. I felt that I was supposed to empty my piggy bank and bring the contents to you. Now I know the reason.' She reached into her purse.

She placed a white envelope on my desk and with an expression of hope that it would be of some help, she thanked me for showing her our Center, and left. That envelope contained just over thirty-two dollars, exactly the amount we needed to feed ourselves for the rest of the day.

And, do you know, that teen-ager's prayer was answered too! For the rest of the summer, we never again wanted for food.

Finding enough money to run the Center was a matter of even greater difficulty. As the time grew closer for our young workers to go back to school, we made a reckoning of what it had cost us to run the Center full swing for the summer. We were astonished at how much cash was involved.

There were monthly mortgage payments, electric bills and food bills, printing bills and transportation bills. There were clothing bills for our street boys, whose clothes we often had to throw away; there were repair bills and plumbing bills and taxes. There were salaries: even the small wages we were paying our workers came to two hundred dollars. The total of all our expenses regularly ran to more than a thousand dollars each week.

And at no time did we have more than just a few dollars in the bank. Usually our balance was less than a hundred dollars. Just as fast as the money came in, we found a pressing need for it. Often I've yearned for a financial situation that would allow us to breathe a little more easily. But just as often, I come back to the conviction that the Lord wants us to live this way. It is one of the most demanding requirements of our faith to depend totally on God for the needs of His work. Just as soon as we have a balance in the bank, we'll stop depending on Him in the day-by-day, hour-by-hour way that we now do, not only for our spiritual needs, but for our physical needs as well.

Where does this thousand dollars a week come from?

A lot of it is raised by the teen-agers themselves. All across the country young boys and girls have taken on the challenge of this work. They help support it. They baby-sit, mow lawns, and wash cars. Hundreds and hundreds of them have pledged fifty cents a week to help other teen-agers like themselves. This money comes in pennies at a time and each penny is blessed and appreciated.

Then there are individual churches across the country who have taken us as a missionary concern. Just the other day we had a lady visiting us from Florida. She had read about Teen Challenge Center, but the full impact of the need in this city did not strike her until we walked with her around one block and explained what she was seeing with her own eyes. Here was an alcoholic young girl; there a male prostitute, aged fifteen; here was a boy who could not break his addiction to heroin, there a boy who was simply lonesome. When she got back to her church she stood before the congregation and told what she had seen. 'Here I live in comfort, while those kids are out there starving for spiritual help. I, for one, am going to make the Center my personal concern. I hope you will join me. They need every cent they can raise.'

All of these sources, however, could never meet the extraordinary requirements of the Center, such as the original financing of the building that had to be taken on as a crisis, handled as a crisis, and turned over to God.

And now, just as we were finally under way, I knew that we were faced with a crisis again.

In two weeks the second mortgage on the home was due: fifteen thousand dollars!

I had, frankly, simply closed my eyes to the approaching deadline for that large payment. Certainly I had not been putting anything aside toward its payment. We were barely scraping by as it was.

August 28, 1961, was our deadline. I knew all too well that we would have to face reality on that date.

Chapter Nineteen

The closer we came to our financial crisis, the more determined I became to find the money, because we were faced with another challenge, on a different plane from any we had faced before.

Late one afternoon Maria telephoned me to say that she wanted to see me.

'Of course, Maria. You have our new address.'

I called Linda in and briefed her about Maria. 'This is a girl you should know,' I said. 'She has tremendous potential if her energies can ever be channelled in the right direction. She's brave; but it's gang bravery. When she became president of her gang she had to stand with her back to the wall and let the kids hit her as hard as they could. She's a brilliant organizer; but she's thrown this away on the gang: she built her unit up until it had more than three hundred girls in it.

'But I don't think she's coming about the gangs; I think she's coming because she's back on heroin.'

Then I briefed Linda on Maria's battle with the drug. I told her how she'd been a mainline addict when I first met her more than four years earlier. I told how she'd tried to throw the habit after she came forward at St Nick's, how she'd married, how everything seemed to go smoothly for a while. Maria quit the gang, Johnny got a job, children began to come along.

But one day Maria and Johnny had a fight. The first thing Maria did was to connect with a seller and start 'drilling' again. She had gone off once more for a short while. But now, I felt sure, she was calling to say she was back on again.

While Linda and I were talking, my secretary came in and told us that Maria was outside. What a tragic change had come over the girl since I last saw her! Linda and I both stood when Maria walked in. It was a strange reaction, a little like the feeling that you should stand in the presence of death.

Maria's eyes were glassy. Her nose ran. Her complexion was mottled and pasty. Her hair was matted and unkempt. Her heels were run over, she had no stockings on and black hair stood out on her legs.

But the thing that struck me most strongly about Maria were her hands. Instead of hanging gracefully at her side, she held her hands as tight fists, slightly raised. She kept clenching and unclenching her fists, as if ready to fight at a single provocation.

'Reverend Wilkerson,' she said, 'I don't need to tell you I need help.'

'Come on in, Maria,' I said. We pulled a chair up for her.

'Sit down,' said Linda. 'Let me get you some tea.'

Poor Linda, she didn't know that a 'tea party' was a heroin addict's slang phrase for a drilling session. She must have been surprised at Maria's fierce reaction.

'No!' she said. 'I don't want anything!' She sat down.

'How are the children?'

'Who should know?'

'You've left Johnny?'

'We fight.'

I looked at Linda. 'I've told Linda about you, Maria. Everything, both good and bad. After we've had a visit, I want you to get to know Linda better. She's working with a lot of girls around the city. I chose her because she's got a real way of understanding. You'll get along.'

Maria and Linda did have their talk. Later Linda came into my office, worried that she had not gotten through at all to the girl.

'It's the drugs, Dave,' she said. 'What a devil-inspired poison! It's death to the installment plan.'

A few days later, matters got worse. Maria called Linda on the telephone. She was pleading for help. She was about to get into serious trouble, she said, and she didn't know how to stop herself. She had just taken her third shot of heroin and she had drunk a full bottle of whiskey, and she and her old gang were heading off to fight a rival gang. 'We're going to kill a girl named Dixie,' Maria said. 'You've got to come stop us.'

Linda and two of her partners raced uptown to 134th Street in Manhattan. They barged right into the headquarters of the girls' gang. They stayed for more than an hour, but before they left the fight was called off.

'Dave,' said Linda when she got back, 'this thing is desperate. We've simply got to do something for these girls.'

What is this thing called drug addiction?

It took me four years to put into focus a picture of the complex threat that lies behind the single word 'narcotics'. But the picture that finally emerged is staggering.

According to the latest official estimates, there are more than 30,000 addicts in New York City alone, and these statistics are based only on the records of those who are hospitalized, jailed or committed to an institution. Thousands of others are 'breaking in' on heroin by sniffing and 'skin popping': thousands of men, women, and children condemned to what Linda vividly called 'death on the installment plan'.

There are enough teen-agers among these addicts to people a small town: at least 4,000! Still more significant, and more frightening, is the fact that the *percentage* of teenage addicts is increasing. And this, of course, takes into account the fact that each year hundreds of addicts leave the ranks of teen-agers by the simple process of growing up.

To understand the threat and the challenge of dope addiction among our teen-agers, it was necessary first for me to gain some understanding of the fantastic profits that are available to the trafficker in narcotics.

By far the most common addictive drug in use in New York is heroin, a derivative of opium. A kilo of heroin can be purchased in Beirut, Lebanon, for $3,000. Smuggled in, sold, re-sold, and cut at each step along the way, the kilo will sell on the streets of the city for $300,000. In time of scarce supply the same $3,000 investment can bring a return of a million! Any trade that can convert $3,000 into a million (tax free) dollars is going to flourish.

Couple these profits with the fact that it is practically impossible to prevent smuggling, and you have the makings of the narcotics trade in New York. It takes a crew of twelve agents the best part of a day to search a single ship for narcotics. There are 12,500 ships arriving from foreign ports each year in New York harbours, and an additional eighteen thousand airplanes. To patrol these thirty thousand carriers, the US Treasury Department, Bureau of Customs, is given a pitiful 265 men. The result is that a man not known as a runner can walk into the city with virtually no risk, carrying a million dollars worth of heroin sewed in little silken bags attached to his garments.

But how do the sellers find a market? Here is the story:

Newspaper headlines recently screamed that dope peddlers were operating just outside the grounds of one of the city's schools. This was no news to school officials. They knew that most addicts got their first sample of narcotics in the immediate neighbourhood of a school. Students at Junior High School 44 in Brooklyn were recently denied the privilege of leaving the school building during their lunch hour. Officials felt this 'captive lunch' was necessary for the protection of the children, so prevalent was dope pushing in the immediate vicinity! Peddlers boldly waited just outside the schoolyard gate, and on occasion actually came into the playground.

These pushers offer samples of their wares free-of-charge.

One boy (Joseph), whom I got to know very, very well, told me how this works.

'A pusher gets you into his car, Davie, and maybe he's got one or two kids from your class in there smoking pot. "Marijuana won't hurt you," they say. Then they tell you it isn't habit-forming. Which it isn't: but marijuana leads to habit-forming drugs. The pusher tries to get you to take a smoke, and if you hesitate, the other boys start to laugh and call you "chicken" and in the end maybe you give in and take one of his cigarettes. That's how I got started.'

Joseph's story is typical. The child takes a puff in the back seat of some pusher's car. He learns that you don't inhale marijuana like you do tobacco; you sniff it until the fumes make you feel giddy. That first day, when the boy returns to school, he is untroubled by his problems. Most narcotics addicts are lonesome, frustrated, angry and usually come from a broken home. One sampling of the wonderful weed and the boy discovers what it would be like to be permanently happy. He forgets his drunken father and wandering mother, he is unruffled by the total lack of love in his life, by the stifling poverty that forces him to sleep in the same bed as his two sisters and in the same room as his parents. He forgets all this. He is free, and that is no small thing.

The next day the obliging pusher is on hand to suggest another little sample of heaven. When the boy is ready, he is introduced to stronger stuff: heroin. Here, too, the pattern is followed: a free gift of the drug the first time, the first two times. The pusher is happy to make the investment because he knows that *only fifteen days of continuous heroin use produces addiction!*

Now comes the truly fiendish part of this story.

Heroin costs from three to fifteen dollars a 'deck' – a deck is a tiny cellophane container of the drug, sufficient for a single intravenous shot.

'Davie,' one twenty-year-old girl told me during a heroin shortage, 'it costs me sixty dollars a day to support my habit. I've heard of users hooked to the tune of a hundred dollars a day.' More typical, I found, would be a twenty-five or thirty-dollars-a-day habit. Where is a teen-ager who is given twenty-five cents a day lunch money going to find twenty-five dollars?

He might turn to crime. Teen-age muggings, purse snatchings, shoplifting, house breaking, armed robbery, auto thefts have become a major problem in New York, and the police say the reason is dope addiction. But the boy gets only one-third of the value of his theft when he sells it to a receiver of stolen goods. So to support a twenty-five-dollar-a-day habit, he must steal seventy-five dollars worth of goods. The director of the Narcotics Bureau in New York, Inspector Edward Carey, estimates that drug addiction is responsible for $200,000,000 a year in stolen goods in this city alone.

Theft, though, is not really the answer for a boy who has become addicted. It takes too much ingenuity and too much effort, and there is always the risk involved. A much simple solution is to become a seller.

On a dark street corner, one night, a teen-age boy told me how this happened to him. Karl is eighteen. He has been mainlining for three years. When he first realized that his habit was going to cost him fifteen dollars a day, then twenty dollars a day, then twenty-five, he went to his supplier and offered to help him sell.

'Oh no, boy. If you want to sell you have to find your own customers.' And in this sentence lies the reason for the steady spread of addiction.

Karl, to pay for his own drugs, pressed narcotics on younger boys. He used the same technique that had been used on him. He passed off the habit as being 'worth the couple bucks it costs'. He chose the more sensitive, hurt, withdrawn boys to pressure. He called them 'chicken' when they wouldn't smoke marijuana. And in the end Karl succeeded in building up a business for himself. Into the chain of ever-widening addiction not one but ten new boys were added.

One of the questions I asked these boys was, 'Why don't you just stop?'

Suppose that a boy did choose to stop. This is what he faces. About two hours after the effect of the final shot wears off, the boy begins withdrawal symptoms. First there is a deep craving which pulls at his body from every pore. Then the boy begins to sweat. He shakes with chills, while his body temperature rises higher and higher. He begins to vomit. He retches for hours on end. His nerves twang with excruciating pain from foot to hair roots. He suffers hallucinations and nightmares more horrible than the worst ever imagined by an alcoholic.

This lasts for three full days. And unless he is helped, he just won't make it. Even *with* help, the chances are nine to one that he will never be free from his habit. Each year 3,500 addicts are admitted to the United States Public Health Service Hospital in Lexington. More than six hundred doctors and staff members try to help the addict free himself from the habit. Yet a twenty-year study, carried out between 1935 and 1955, showed that sixty-four per cent of the addicts returned! Many more went back on drugs without returning to the hospital. Between eighty-five and ninety per cent of the addicts, says Dr Murray Diamond, Chief Medical Officer at the hospital, eventually return to their habit.

'Once you are hooked, man,' a boy who had been to Lexington told me, 'you are hooked for good. I got me a fix within five minutes after getting out of that place.'

What happens to the nine out of ten addicts who cannot throw their habit? A physical deterioration takes place that is painful and repelling. Karl, even while he was pushing drugs upon younger boys, had in his possession an official bulletin from the New York Police Department describing the effects on the body of continued use of drugs:

> To be a confirmed drug addict is to be one of the walking dead. There are many symptoms to indicate a confirmed addict – any of them may be present:
> The teeth had rotted out; the appetite is lost and the stomach and intestines don't function

properly. The gall bladder becomes inflamed; eyes and skin turn a bilious yellow. In some cases the membranes of the nose turn a flaming red; the partition separating the nostrils is eaten away – breathing is difficult. Oxygen in the blood decreases; bronchitis and tuberculosis develop. Good traits of character disappear and bad ones emerge. Sex organs become affected. Veins collapse and livid purplish scars remain. Boils and abscesses plague the skin; gnawing pain racks the body. Nerves snap; vicious twitching develops. Imaginary and fantastic fears blight the mind and sometimes complete insanity results. Oftentimes, too, death comes – much too early in life. Compared with normal persons, according to one authority quoted in a US Treasury Department pamphlet, drug addicts die of tuberculosis at a rate of four to one; pneumonia, two to one; premature old age, five to one; bronchitis, four to one; brain haemorrhage, three to one; and more than two to one of a wide variety of other diseases. Such is the torment of being a drug addict; such is the plague of being one of the walking dead.

Karl knew what was ahead for him. It didn't slow him down at all. Nor did it slow Shorty down. Shorty came to me looking for help, and in the process he taught me a tragic lesson.

Shorty was nineteen years of age, and addicted to heroin. He had been on drugs since he was fifteen years old. Tammy was Shorty's girlfriend, a very beautiful girl of seventeen. Her parents were known in New York business and social circles, and attended a fashionable church.

Shorty asked me to 'get Tammy off the stuff', and I agreed to see the girl. When Shorty and I tapped on the door of a dark, rat-infested back-street tenement basement-room in Brooklyn, there was a quick shuffling inside. We waited, while an impatient Shorty mumbled under his breath. When the door opened, there stood Tammy, open-mouthed in surprise at our sudden visit.

There were two other young men in the dimly lit room; they had rolled up the sleeves of their left arms. On the table before them lay the 'works' consisting of a needle, bottle cap 'cooker', a glass of water and a small cellophane bag containing a white substance, 'H' or 'horse' or heroin.

'Who's he!' said Tammy, jerking her head toward me.

'He's okay,' said Shorty. 'He's a preacher. I asked him to come here.'

'Well, he's going to have to wait if he wants to talk to me.' Tammy turned her back on us and went ahead with the heating process we had interrupted. Shorty must have read my mind, because he turned to me and whispered very softly,

'Don't try to stop them, Preach. If you mess up the fix, those boys'll kill you. I mean that. If you go out and try to get the cops, we'll be gone by the time you get back. Stick around. It's good for your education.'

So I stuck around and got my education in what it's like to be a teen-ager on dope.

While the preparation of the injection was going on, Shorty told me Tammy's story. She, too, had been on heroin since she was fifteen. Her parents didn't know the double life she led, including the nights she spent with men. All they knew was that Tammy had left home and was living in the Village. They saw her on weekends and, although they were a little shocked at Tammy's Bohemian life, still all girls had to go through the rebel stage. They left her alone.

Tammy's rebel stage consisted of growing addiction to heroin, and a deepening involvement in sex-for-pay. 'She has to do it to support her habit,' said Shorty. 'She's a call girl. She has a regular list of clients, most of them Madison Avenue businessmen with wives up in Westchester.' And then Shorty lowered his voice. 'But the thing that gets me is how she's taken up with these queers. She's becoming more and more a lesbian. It's where she gets her kicks.'

I didn't have the heart to ask Shorty where he fitted into this picture. He was less than five feet tall, and dark. Tammy was slender, tall and blonde. I just let the subject alone. Shorty was getting impatient.

I shall never be the same, as a result of the scene I witnessed in the next few moments. The preparation of the fix had taken some little time. By now each teen-ager, including Shorty, was pushing and struggling to shoot up first. The sickest was allowed to drill before the others, and Shorty suddenly went into a seizure of shaking and retching and moaning. I suppose so that he could be first. With starving eyes the four youngsters watched one of the boys pour heroin from the little cellophane bag into the cap cooker. Not one grain was wasted.

'Hurry up,' they all screamed, low, into his ear.

With shaking hands the boy lit two matches under the cooker and boiled the contents. The other addict took off his belt and applied a tourniquet to Shorty's arm. The other addicts were now getting very agitated. They stood by gritting their teeth and clenching their fists to keep from grabbing the loaded needle from Shorty's hand. Tears were streaming down their cheeks, they were cursing under their breath and biting their lips.

And then, one by one, there was that final puncture that was so exhilarating: needle against extended vein.

I have never felt so close to hell. The kids drifted off into a kind of euphoria. For a long, long time I listened to their foolish gossip and rambling. Shorty told me of a dream, where he stood before mountains of white H, loaded needles and an eternal fire to boil the stuff with. That seemed to him like pure heaven, a place where he could shoot mountains of heroin into his veins.

'What about it, Preach? You going to get Tammy off the stuff?' Shorty asked, suddenly remembering why he had asked me in.

I told him I would certainly try. And I did try to talk with Tammy then and there, but she looked at me with glassy eyes and told me to go to hell. What could I offer that she didn't have right now, she said. She was in heaven. I just didn't know what heaven was like. She could handle herself without any help from a screwball preacher.

Shorty, too, thought better of having invited me in now that he had his fix. When I told him that I had no magic cure, that all I could offer was help while he went cold turkey, he looked at me and scratched his head and said, 'Well, what'd you come here for, then . . .?'

So I failed.

I failed as I had with Maria. I left the apartment. When I went back to try to help them again, Tammy and Shorty had disappeared. All their gear was gone. Nobody knew where they were. Nor did anybody seem to care.

Chapter Twenty

The tremendous hold that drugs have on the human body cannot be explained in physical terms alone. My grandfather would say that the devil had these boys in his grip, and I think my grandfather is right. The boys themselves say this, but in a different way:

'Davie,' I was told over and again, 'there are two habits you've got to kick if you're hooked. The body habit, and the mind habit. The body habit's not too much or a problem: you just stay in sheer hell for three days, put up with a little less torture for another month, and you're free.

'But that mind habit, Davie . . . that's something terrible! There's a thing inside you that *makes* you come back. Something spooky, whispering to you. We got names for this guy: either he's a monkey on our back, or a vulture on our veins.

'We can't get rid of him, Davie. But you're a preacher. Maybe this Holy Spirit you talk about, maybe He can help.'

I don't know why it took so long for me to realize that this was, indeed, the direction we should take. The realization came about as an evolution, starting with a failure and ending with a magnificent discovery.

The failure was a boy named Joe. I'll never forget the four traumatic days I spent with him, trying to bring him through the pain of withdrawing from an addiction to heroin.

Joe was such a nice guy. Tall, blond, at one time a good athlete in high school, he had not come into his addiction by the usual route.

'I suppose those pain-killers were necessary,' Joe told me in my office at the Center. 'I know that when I needed them I was glad for the relief they brought. But look what happened to me afterwards. I never broke away.'

Joe told me the story. He had been working for a coal company. One day he slipped and fell down a chute. The accident put him in the hospital for several months, and for most of that time Joe was in severe pain. To help relieve his agony, the doctor prescribed a narcotic. By the time Joe was released from the hospital he was addicted.

'I couldn't get any more of the drug,' he told me. 'But I discovered that there was a kind of cough syrup that had narcotics in it and I started walking all over the city buying it. I'd have to go to a different drugstore each time and use a fake name, but I didn't have any trouble getting all I wanted. I used to step into the nearest bathroom and down a whole eight-ounce bottle at once.'

After a while even this didn't satisfy Joe's growing need for drugs. He knew that some of his old high school buddies were using heroin, and he got in touch with them. From then on the pattern was typical. First sniffing, then skin popping, then mainline injections. When Joe came to us, he had been on heroin for more than eight months. He was deeply addicted.

'Can you stay here at the Center for three or four days?' I asked.

'No one else wants me.'

'You can live upstairs with the workers.'

Joe shrugged.

'It won't be easy, you know. You'll be going off cold turkey.'

Joe shrugged again.

Cold turkey – instantaneous withdrawal – is the method usually used in jails to take a boy off narcotics. We used it partly because we had no choice: we could not administer the withdrawal drugs they use in hospitals. But we prefer cold turkey on its own merits, too. The withdrawal is considerably faster: three days as against three weeks. The pain is more intense, but it is over sooner.

So we brought Joe to the Center and gave him a room upstairs with the men workers. How glad I was that we had a registered nurse living at the home. Barbara Culver's room was just under Joe's. She'd keep an eye on him all the time he was with us. We also put a doctor on the alert in case we should need him.

'Joe,' I said, as soon as we had him settled in, 'as of this moment the withdrawal has started. I can promise you that you won't be alone for one second. When we aren't with you in person, we will be with you in prayer.'

We weren't just going to take the boy off drugs and leave him alone to suffer. The entire four days would be coupled with an intensive, supportive prayer campaign. Prayer would be said for him around the clock. Day and night boys and girls would be in the chapel interceding for him. Others would be with him in person upstairs reading Scripture to him.

One of the first things we had to do with Joe was break the expectation of pain. Instantaneous withdrawal is bad enough by itself, without the added handicap of expecting it to be hell. I asked Joe where he got the idea the withdrawal was going to be so rough.

'Well . . . gee . . . everyone says . . .'

'That's just it. Everyone says it's rough, so you're sitting here sweating just at the thought of what's ahead. As a matter of fact, that need not be the case at all.' And I told Joe about a boy I knew who had been on marijuana and on heroin and who had been released instantaneously, without any of the withdrawal symptoms. That was rare, I admitted, and Joe had to be prepared for a rough time. But why make it any worse than it had to be? We worked hard to help Joe separate the real symptoms from the psychological symptoms that came from apprehension.

Then we had Joe learn the thirty-first Psalm.

This is a wonderful Psalm. We call it the Song of the Drug Addict. There are certain verses in particular that are just made for their condition:

Pull me out of the net that they have laid priv-
ily for me: for Thou art my strength.

Have mercy upon me. O Lord, for I am in trouble; mine
eye is consumed with grief, yea, my soul and my belly.

For my life is spent with grief, and my years with sigh-
ing: my strength faileth because of mine iniquity, and
my bones are consumed.

I was a reproach among all mine enemies, but especially
among my neighbours, and a fear to mine acquaintance;
they that did see me without fled from me.
I am forgotten as a dead man out of mind: I am
like a broken vessel.

Once the real withdrawal pains began, Joe stayed up
there in his room while he sweated through the symptoms.
Barbara checked his condition regularly. I hated to go into that
room. Joe lay on the bed gripping his stomach as the cramps hit
him again and again. His body was a high flushed pink. Sweat
poured off him in little rivers that left the bed soaked through
to the mattress. He cried out in his pain and pounded his head
with his hands. He wanted water, then threw it up. He pleaded
with me to help him, and all I could do was hold his hand and
promise him that we cared.

At night we set up a tape recorder by Joe's bed and
played Scripture readings to him. I stayed at the Center during
this trial. Often during the dead of night I would slip into the

chapel to be sure someone was always there, then up the stairs to see how Joe was doing. The recorder was softly repeating portions of the Bible to the boy as he tossed in fitful sleep. Never once during those three days and nights did the torment let up. It was a terror to watch.

Then, on the fourth day, Joe seemed much better.

He walked around the Center smiling wanly and saying that he thought maybe the worst was over. All of us were happy with him. When Joe said he wanted to go home to see his parents, I was a little dubious, but there was nothing we could do to detain the boy if he wanted to leave.

And so, smiling and thankful, Joe walked out the front door of the Center and turned down Clinton Avenue.

It came time for him to return. No Joe.

The next morning we learned that our Joe had been arrested for robbery and for possession of narcotics.

That was our failure. 'What went wrong?' I asked at a staff meeting. 'The boy went through the rough part. He got all the way through the worst three days he would ever have to spend. He had a tremendous investment to protect. And he threw it all over.'

'Why don't you talk to the boys who have come off successfully?' said Howard Culver. 'Maybe you'll find the key.'

There were several such boys I wanted to talk to. One by one I called them in and listened to their stories of deliverance. And they all spoke of a common experience.

I spoke to Nicky, who had been taking goof balls and smoking marijuana. I asked him when it was that he felt he had victory over his old way of life. Something tremendous had happened to him, he said, at the time of his conversion on the street corner. He had been introduced at that time to the love of God. But it wasn't until later that he knew he had complete victory.

'And when was that, Nicky?'

'At the time of my baptism in the Holy Spirit.'

I called in David and asked him the same thing. When did he feel that he had power over himself? 'Oh, I can answer that,' said David. 'When I was baptized in the Holy Spirit.'

Again and again I got the same report. I cannot describe how excited I was. A pattern seemed to be emerging. I felt that I was on the verge of something tremendous.

Chapter Twenty-One

What is the baptism of the Holy Spirit?

Shortly after we became interested in the Holy Spirit's role in helping a boy rid himself of an addiction to narcotics, we had a visit at the Center from a Jesuit priest. He, too, wanted to know more about the baptism. He had heard our young people at a street rally and was so impressed that he wanted to know their secret.

We spent an afternoon with Father Gary at the Center, exploring with him the deep meanings of the baptism. The first thing we did was to show him the references to the experience in the Douay version of the Bible. 'The baptism of the Holy Spirit is not a denominational experience,' I said. 'We have Episcopalians and Lutherans and Baptists and Methodists working with us, all of whom have been filled with the Holy Spirit.'

In its essence, we told Father Gary, the baptism is a religious experience which gives you power. 'But you will receive power when the Holy Spirit comes upon you,' said Jesus when He showed Himself to His apostles after His death.

In my office, Father Gary and I bent over the Bible. 'The first reference to this special experience comes in the early part of the Gospel story. The Jews, you remember, wondered for a while if John the Baptist were the Messiah. But John told them, "There cometh one mightier than I after me, the latchet of whose shoes I am not worthy to stoop down and unloose. I indeed," he said, and this is the important prediction, "I indeed have baptized you with water; but he shall baptize you with the Holy Ghost."[1]

From the beginning of Christianity, then, this baptism of the Holy Ghost has had a special significance because it marks the difference between the mission of a mere man, no matter how bold and effective, and the mission of Christ: Jesus would baptize His followers with the Holy Ghost. In His last hours on earth, Jesus spent a great deal of time talking to His disciples about the Holy Ghost who would come after His death to stand by them, comfort them, lead them and give them that power which would allow them to carry His mission forward.

Then, after the crucifixion, He appeared to them and told them not to leave Jerusalem. 'You must wait,' He said, 'for the promise made by my Father, about which you have heard me speak: John, as you know, baptized with water, but you will be baptized with the Holy Spirit, and within the next few days . . . you will receive power when the Holy Spirit comes upon you.'[2]

And then we turned to the second chapter of Acts. 'It was immediately after this,' I reminded Father Gary, 'that the disciples were gathered together in Jerusalem to celebrate Pentecost. "While the day of Pentecost was running its course they were all together in one place, when suddenly there came from the sky a noise like that of a strong driving wind, which filled the whole house where they were sitting. And there appeared to them tongues like flames of fire, dispersed among them and resting on each one. And they were all filled with the Holy Spirit and began to talk in other tongues, as the Spirit gave them power of utterance."[3]

'This experience at Pentecost is where we Pentecostals get our name. We place a tremendous store in the baptism of the Holy Spirit as it was foretold by John, promised by the Father and

---

[1]Mark 1:7-8
[2]Acts 1:4-8 (New English Bible)
[3]Acts 2:2-4 (New English Bible)

experienced at Pentecost. I'm sure you've noticed the vast change that took place in the apostles after this experience. Before, they had been timid and powerless men. Afterwards, they did receive that power that Christ spoke about. They healed the sick, cast out demons, raised the dead. The same men who had hidden themselves at the crucifixion went on after this experience to stand up to the hostile world with their message.'

Then I told Father Gary about the gigantic revival which swept the United States, Canada, England, and South America in the early 1900s. At the heart of this revival was the message that the power given to the Church at Pentecost had for the most part fallen into impotency, and could be brought back through the baptism of the Holy Spirit. 'The Book of Acts tells of five different times when people received this experience,' I said, 'and the early Pentecostals noticed that in four out of five of these times, the people who were baptized with the Holy Spirit began to "speak in other tongues."'

Father Gary wanted to know what speaking in other tongues was like. 'It's like talking in another language. A language that you don't understand.' One by one I pointed out to Father Gary the places in the Bible where this experience followed the baptism of the Holy Spirit. The disciples spoke in tongues at Pentecost; Saul was filled with the Holy Spirit after his Damascus Road conversion and subsequently spoke in tongues, saying, 'I thank my God, I speak in tongues more than ye all';[4] the members of Cornelius' household were baptized with the Holy Spirit and began to speak in tongues; the new Christians at Ephesus were similarly baptized and began to speak in tongues. 'Even in the story of the fifth baptism, at Samaria, Simon the Magician saw something so extraordinary happen that he wanted the power himself and offered money for it, "that when I lay my hands on anyone, he will receive the Holy Spirit."[5] Doesn't it seem logical that the experience he saw was also speaking in tongues?'

---

[4]1 Cor. 14:18
[5]Acts 8:19

'That would make sense I suppose if it happened in all the other baptisms. When did you have the experience yourself?'

'It's been a tradition in our family for three generations.'

And then we talked a while about my wonderful, fiery old grandfather. He first heard this message in 1925. He preached against it, too, at every occasion he could find.

'But then one day,' I recounted, 'while he was in the pulpit preaching against the Pentecostals, he himself began to tremble and shake, which is one of the things that happens often when people first have this power flow into them. It's something you feel, a little like a shock, except that the sensation is not at all unpleasant. Anyhow, Grandpa was the most surprised person in the world when this happened to him, and he himself received the baptism and began to speak in tongues. From that day on he preached Pentecost whenever and wherever he could, because he saw personally what power the experience held. My father received it when he was twenty-five, and I received it when I was only thirteen; all three generations of us preach this message today.'

Father Gary wanted to know what the actual experience was like.

'Why don't you ask the kids?' I said. We invited him to have lunch with us, and over chicken and salad, Father Gary listened as several of our young people described for him what it had been like when they were filled with the Spirit.

The first was a twelve-year-old girl named Neda. We have found her in Coney Island, wandering around as if lost. Linda Meisner learned from her that sex and alcohol were the centres of her revolt against her family. 'I used to drink a lot,' she said now, 'and to run around with any boy who looked that way at me. I hated my parents, especially my mother. Linda brought me here to the Center and I sat in the chapel and listened to all the other kids talk about how Jesus helped them when they were tempted. When I had problems, like being with a boy, I used to break up and get disgusted, but these dope addicts had problems, too, worse than mine. "We still get tempted," they say, "but now we always run into the chapel and pray." When they prayed, they spoke in another language but they looked happy and were sure of themselves. And when they got up from their knees, their temptation was gone.

'So they made me want the same thing. I went into the chapel one day to pray by myself. I started telling God all about my problems and I asked Him to come into my life like He had to those drug addicts. Like a blinding light, Jesus burst into my heart. Something took over my speech. It made me feel like I was sitting down by a river that somehow was flowing through me and bubbled up out of me like a musical language. It was after this that one of the workers showed me in the Book of Acts what it was all about. It was the most wonderful thing that ever happened.'

Father Gary just sat listening and nodding his head and sometimes saying, 'Yes, yes,' in recognition of what she was saying.

The next boy especially brought this reaction from Father Gary. 'First of all,' said John, 'I know this is real. And you know how? Because afterward Jesus Christ seemed to come right out of the Bible. He became a living person who wanted to stand with me through my problems.'

'Yes,' said Father Gary. 'This is wonderful.'

'With me,' said a boy named Joseph, 'He helped me get rid of drugs. I used goof balls and marijuana, and I was beginning to skin pop heroin. I already had the mind habit and I had to do this thing. When I heard about Jesus it kind of shocked me that He loved people in spite of all their sins. It stirred me when I heard that He puts real teeth behind His promises, by coming into us with this baptism of the Holy Spirit. The Holy Spirit is called the Comforter, they told me. When I thought of comfort I thought of a bottle of wine and half-a-dozen goof balls. But these guys were talking about comfort out of Heaven where I could feel clean later.

'So I got to wanting this, just like Neda. In the chapel,'
he turned his head toward the door of the chapel, 'I cried to God
for help, and that's when He came around. He took over my lips
and tongue and I was speaking in a new language. At first I
thought I was crazy, but all of a sudden I knew I couldn't be,
because something was happening too. I wasn't lonely any
more. I didn't want any more drugs. I loved everybody. For the
first time in my life I felt clean.'

On and on the kids went, each wanting to tell what had
happened to him. You had to make them take turns talking.
When Father Gary left an hour later, he was still saying, 'Yes,
yes!' He said he wanted to talk the experience over with some of
his friends at Fordham University. I only wish he had stayed a little longer because that same night another boy received the baptism, and he could have witnessed the experience for himself.

The boy's name was Roberto. Roberto was sixteen years
old; he had been on heroin for two years, and on marijuana
before that; he had been in jail four times, once for stabbing
another gang member in a street fight. The boy had lived, but
Roberto was afraid that some day he might kill. Unlike many
of the boys who come to the Center, Roberto had parents who
stood by him. They tried everywhere to get help, but Roberto's
downhill slide only increased its pace.

That afternoon I met Roberto in the chapel. I guessed
from the way he was fidgeting and moving around restlessly
that he was about to go out for a fix.

'I've got problems, Davie,' he said, quietly lacing and
unlacing his fingers. When an addict says he has problems, he
means that he has to make contact and shoot it up – and soon.

So I started talking to Roberto again about the baptism
of the Holy Spirit. 'Nicky will be preaching about it tonight. Be
there, and let the Spirit come upon you.'

'I don't know, Davie. I've got to get some fresh air. I'm
not feeling so good.'

I had to let him go, and frankly I didn't expect to see him again. But that night he was in the chapel when I arrived. I could tell from the way he continued to suffer that he had made it without getting a fix. I sat down beside him, and watched him carefully as several of our ex-gang members and drug addicts arose and quite simply told of the wondrous things that were happening to them. Nicky preached about the need of every drug addict to have the baptism of the Holy Spirit.

'If you want power in your life . . . if you are on the needle and really want to change, then listen to this. The Holy Spirit is what you need. And when you receive Him, you will also receive ten special gifts which you can depend on. I'm going to tell you about them. If you have a pencil and paper you can copy down the Bible references that show where I got them.

'First of all you have power. You can read that in Acts 1:8. You shall have power when the Holy Spirit comes upon you.

'Then, you're going to have a Comforter. John 14:26. A Comforter doesn't mean someone who will make you comfortable, it means someone who will stand by you and give you strength.

'Next you will have protection. Read in Acts 16:6 how the Holy Spirit forbids the apostles to take a step which would have been tragic. He will guide you like this, too.

'And here's an important one: you will no longer be hounded by the mind of the flesh, but you will have spiritual values. Read it in Ephesians 2:3-6.

'You will have life. Now you are headed for death, but with the Holy Spirit, it says in Second Corinthians 3:5-6 that you will have new life.

'And you will be living with the Spirit of Truth. The needle holds out a promise to you that is never fulfilled. You don't get release in a drilling session, it just gets worse. John 16:13 tells you that you will have Truth.

'Access to the Father will be yours. Read Ephesians 2:18.

'And the last three: You will have Hope. How many of you have that now? Not many. You will have Hope, says Romans 15:13.

'And the point of all this is found in Second Corinthians 3:17. You, you boys out there now, will have liberty!

'And how does this come about? Through a dramatic, sudden, overpowering experience. Read about it for yourselves in Acts 10:44.'

Then Nicky stopped. His voice dropped and he spoke in almost a whisper. 'That's what's ahead for you in this new life,' he said. 'But here tonight I don't think we want to *read* about it. And we don't want to *talk* about it. We want to *do* it!

'If you want this change and power and hope and freedom in your life, get on your feet and come up front. I'm going to lay my hands on your head just like St Paul did and the same thing is going to happen to you that happened to the new Christians in his time. You're going to receive the Holy Spirit!'

Roberto took one look at me and leapt to his feet; and my heart leapt with him.

'I want everything God has for me,' he said. 'I want to make it through and never come back.'

Roberto fairly ran to the front of the chapel. He grabbed Nicky's hands and put them on his own head. Almost immediately the same thing happened to this boy that had happened to my grandfather; he began to tremble as if current were flowing through him. He fell to his knees, and the other boys stood around him, praying.

It was like reliving a scene from the Book of Acts. In less than two minutes a new language was flowing from Roberto's lips. It poured out like a spring bubbling up out of dry land. Of course, everyone was rejoicing. All the other drug addicts came around Nicky and Roberto and began saying, 'He's going to make it. He's coming through.' Nicky kept saying, 'Thank You, Lord. Thank You for helping these boys.'

Then others picked it up.

'Thank You, Lord. Thank You for helping these boys.'

'Thank You. Thank You. Thank You, Lord.'

Chapter Twenty-Two

We did not find that the baptism of the Holy Spirit always freed a boy. In fact, it did just the opposite: it trapped him.

This has been simultaneously one of the most discouraging, and the most encouraging, results of our work. At first our hopes were very high that the baptism would always, and permanently, free boys from the hold of heroin.

There was a good basis for this hope. As soon as we began to suspect that there was a relationship between the baptism and a boy's ability to throw the habit, we made a special effort to lead our young dope addicts into the experience.

At first we experimented, rather cautiously, on a marijuana user. Luis was one of our boys who had been smoking this weed, which addicts the mind but not the body. He received the baptism of the Holy Spirit, and his mind addiction left him completely.

Encouraged, we went on to a tougher assignment. What about a boy like Roberto, who had been on heroin, which addicts the mind and the body as well? What would happen to him now? We watched Roberto carefully for signs that he was back on the drugs, but day after day he came to the Center with his eyes shining and his hopes high. 'I think I'm on top of it, David. I have a tool I can use; I just come here with the other boys and pray.'

Time and again we got the same results. Harvey had been referred to us by the courts; he had been deeply addicted to heroin for three years, but after the baptism he said the temptation itself went away. Johnny had been on heroin four years, and pulled away successfully after his baptism. Lefty had used the needle two years, and after his baptism he not only stopped drugs, he decided to go into the ministry. Vincent used heroin two years, until his baptism when he stopped instantaneously. Ruben had a four-year addiction; at his baptism he was given the power to stop. Eddie had started on heroin when he was twelve years old; fifteen years later he was still using the drug, and was nearly dead from its continual use. The baptism of the Holy Spirit released him from his addiction.

I was so excited that I checked with medical authorities to find out what grounds we had for making some bold claims. 'None,' I was told frankly. 'At Lexington, a boy is not considered cured until he has been off the stuff five years. How long have your boys been clean?'

'Not long.'

'Just a few days?'

'Oh no, it's a matter of months. In a few cases over a year.'

'Well, that's encouraging. Tell me some more. I'd like to know about this baptism of yours.'

At the end of our interview, I was warned again that a drug addict is virtually impossible to help, and that I should be on the lookout for a fall. 'And the sad part is,' I was told, 'when a boy slips, he goes back to a deeper addiction than before. If he was shooting twice, he'll go to three. If three, he'll skip to five. The degeneration is more rapid after a fall.'

And then one of the boys did slip. Even after the baptism of the Holy Spirit. He had not learned that *living* in the Spirit is as necessary as *receiving* the Spirit.

Ralph had been on marijuana for two years and on heroin for three years. He was deep into the habit. He had tried a hundred times to break the addiction. He tried to leave his gang, where his buddies were mainlining with him. Each time he failed. There was only one out, Ralph thought: he had to take his own life before he took the life of someone else on a dark night when he was desperate for a fix. One night two years ago, Ralph climbed on a roof. He stood at the ledge, ready to dive head first into the street. He was waiting only until the sidewalk below him was clear.

And at that moment, he heard the sound of singing.

It came from one of our Gang Churches, meeting in a building directly across the street from the tenement where Ralph stood. He lifted his head and listened. 'On a hill far away stood an old rugged cross . . .'

Ralph stepped down from his perch. He listened to the rest of the song, and then he walked down the stairs of the building and crossed the street. A sign outside invited him to come in and hear the story of how God was working in Brooklyn streets to help boys addicted to drugs and tied to the gangs.

He went in. And Ralph has never been the same since. He turned his life over to Christ, and later he received the baptism of the Spirit.

We were very, very proud of Ralph, and we still are. He went off the needle for over a year. He left New York and went out to California to live, and all that while he was clean. Then, he came back and paid us a visit. He was all right for several days, but I noticed a despondency settle over him whenever he returned to his old neighbourhood. I learned that his friends were taunting him about the needle. Ralph was being tempted again. We tried to keep in close touch with him, but Ralph was elusive.

And then he fell. He made contact, and went up to his room and stuck the needle in his veins.

Five times, before Ralph received the baptism of the Holy Spirit, he had tried to pull off drugs. Each time he was so disgusted with himself after falling that he started to drill more heavily than ever. Now he had been off over a year and drilling again.

But a strange thing happened this time. The shot did not have its usual effect. The next day Ralph crept into the Center and asked for me. When he came into my office, he closed the door, and I guessed that he had been drilling.

'Something funny's happened, Davie,' Ralph said, after he finally found courage to tell me what he had done. 'After I got through drilling, it was like I hadn't had anything at all. It wasn't anything like what I'd felt before. I felt something else, though. I suddenly had this strong urge to run to the nearest church and pray. And that's what I did. Davie, this time I was forgiven, and I didn't feel disgusted like before. Instead of going from bad to worse, the temptation just went away.'

Ralph's eyes shone as he said the next words. 'Do you know what I think? I think I'm trapped, all right. But not by heroin. I think I'm trapped by the Holy Spirit. He's in me and won't let me get away.'

Ralph came back to us humbled and fully aware of the fact that the baptism had made him Christ's in a special way. He couldn't get away from Him even when he tried. The same thing was true of Roberto (a different Roberto, who had been drilling for fifteen years), who slipped for a short while but found he couldn't go back to the needle. And for Sonny, who after he slipped once, came back with such fervour and such conviction that he wants to go to seminary.

Where does this leave us?

Certainly we cannot claim a magical cure for dope addiction. The devil which hides in that needle is so deadly strong that any such claim would be folly. All we can say, perhaps, is that we have found a power which captures a boy more strongly than narcotics. But that power is the Holy Spirit Himself which, unlike narcotics, does a strange thing for our boys: He captures only to liberate.

We are still in the infancy of what we consider a bold experiment. We have much to learn about what this religious experience can and cannot do in unhappy lives. Every day we are making new discoveries. Every day we learn how to make our role more effective, how to increase our percentage of permanent cures.

One of the promises of Christ was that His Spirit would lead us into all truth. It is on this promise that we take our stand, knowing that some day He will lead us to principles that can be used not only here on Clinton Avenue but all over the United States, wherever loneliness and despair have led boys and girls to seek release from their problems with a syringe, a dirty needle and a bottle-cap cooker.

———

One day Linda and I were sitting in my office discussing these things and wondering where they might lead us. Yet I was aware that there was one name neither one of us was mentioning: Maria.

'Do you think Maria could ever receive the baptism?' I asked suddenly. I saw in Linda's eyes that she had been wondering the same thing. Together we agreed that Maria had a most difficult problem. She had been on heroin for years. The last time she had come to see us, neither Linda nor I thought she had long to live. Even now I sometimes saw in my sleep the deep, sunken eyes, the clenched fists, the shaking lips.

But we agreed to pray for a miracle in Maria's life. Both of us nursed the dream of guiding her into the baptism there at the Center. But it wasn't to come that way. One day, late in summer, we got a telephone call from uptown. It was Maria, and she was in Reverend Ortez' church.

'Reverend Wilkerson!' she nearly shouted into the phone. 'I got the wonderful news! Last night here I received the Holy Ghost!' She could hardly talk for excitement, so I asked her to put Reverend Ortez on the phone. As he described the event, I could just see the scene: Maria walking into the former private home sandwiched in between apartments where noisy parties were so often held; Maria working her way through other Spanish men and women until she found an empty folding chair; Maria listening to the preaching and hearing the altar call; Maria going forward. I could even hear her voice, so husky the last time she visited us, now begging the Lord to send His Spirit to dwell in her.

I could see her sink to her knees and feel the hope in her heart as warm hands were laid on her head. And then the soft, melodic, bubbling language which she did not understand, coming from her own throat, the seal and sign that prayer had been answered. Reverend Ortez was jubilant. 'We've all waited a long, long time for this, haven't we?' he said.

'Indeed we have. It's another victory.'

Secretly, though, I was filled with apprehension. I knew that Maria had one great weakness. When she got angry, she went back to the needle. It was the pattern many addicts followed, but I had watched it with Maria so many times. I had the feeling that if, just once, she could conquer this problem of anger, she would be all right. And it wasn't long before Maria was put to this very test.

One evening, late, Maria stepped off a bus on an apparently deserted street in Manhattan, near her old turf. From out of the shadows stepped three girls.

'Hi there, Maria.'

Maria turned. She recognized the girls as members of the old gang. She greeted them warmly. In the dark behind them, she recognized, too, the form of a boy.

'Say, Maria,' one of the girls said, 'we hear you're off H. We hear you've got religion now.'

'That's right,' said Maria.

'Well, now, ain't that just wonderful? If you're not having to spend all that money on horse, you must be rolling. I wonder if you'd lend a couple of old friends a dollar or two.'

Maria knew what the money would go for. Many were the times she had sat in a darkened room with these same girls, twisting a belt around her arm and pumping a syringe full of heroin into her veins.

'I'm sorry,' she said. 'Not for what you're going to use the money. I know . . .'

Maria never saw the blow coming. A girl's fist plunged into her stomach. Maria doubled over. Her first instinct was to fight back, and Maria was known all over the area for her fierce fighting strength. But she stood there, hands at her sides. Like the first day when she passed her test for the presidency of the club, Maria took punishment without resisting, without whimpering.

But what a heroic difference between the two occasions. This time Maria was praying.

She was praying, too, when the knife went into her side. She was praying while the threesome leaned over her prone body and grabbed her purse and ran, laughing, down the street.

After a while, Maria stood up, slowly, in the lonesome street. She made her way home, somehow, where Johnny helped her take off her bloodstained clothes. Together they examined the wound. The knife had pierced her flesh close to the ribs. The wound wasn't deep, and Johnny didn't think it would be serious.

What he did worry about was Maria's emotions over the incident. What would happen to her now? Far too often he had watched his wife come along the road to recovery just so far, then slip when something made her angry.

But that night, after she had bathed her bruises and put bandages on the knife cut, Maria fell asleep with the peace of a child.

I was tremendously impressed with this story. Maria paid us a visit at the Center a few days after her beating. She walked in with the black and blue markings of her bruises still livid.

'They messed me up a bit, Reverend Wilkerson. But I just prayed and everything was all right. The Holy Spirit was with me.'

I looked at Linda, who was as astonished as I at the change. 'That's all we need to know,' I said aloud.

The last time I saw Maria, she and her family were on their way to Puerto Rico. Johnny stood proudly at her side. Maria's three young children hung shyly to her freshly starched skirt, and they were clinging to a mother they were beginning to feel they could trust. Maria's hair had just been shampooed and set, and it gleamed in the sun. Her shoes were new. Her legs (perhaps a minister shouldn't be noticing this) were shapely and clean shaven. And (a more appropriate observation) her hands hung relaxed and graceful at her side.

Maria told me that she and her family were going to Puerto Rico for the special purpose of attending a Spanish training school which will equip the couple for full-time work with the church. When they finish their training, they will return to New York where we hope they will work with us here in the Center.

As I stood watching this family disappear I found myself repeating over and over again the words of Jesus, 'Ye shall know the truth, and the truth shall set you free.'

Chapter Twenty-Three

For most people in Brooklyn, the morning of August 28, 1961, was just another bright, hot summer morning. But for us at Teen Challenge Center, the day was dark.

That noon we were supposed to hand over a certified check to the holders of our second mortgage. The amount needed was $15,000.

'How much money do we have in the bank?' I asked Paul DiLena.

'I don't even want to tell you.'

'How much?'

'Fourteen dollars.'

I had been counting so much on another miracle. Somehow in my heart I had confidence that we weren't going to lose the Center, and yet here we were at our deadline and there was no money.

Noon came and went, and still there was no miracle.

I had to ask myself serious questions about my own confidence. Was it just self-delusion? Had I expected too much of God without doing enough myself?

'At least,' I said to Julius Fried, our attorney, 'I'm not going down without a scrap. Could you arrange for an extension?'

Julius spent the afternoon poring over documents and signing papers, and when he had finished his day's work, he announced that he had succeeded in getting an extension.

'They've agreed to wait until September 10, David,' Julius said. 'But if the money isn't in their hands by that time, they will start foreclosure proceedings. Do you have any ideas?'

'Yes,' I said, and Julius' face lit up. But it fell again when I explained just what that idea was. 'I'm going to pray about it,' I said. Julius was accustomed to the praying ways of the Center, but at that moment I think he wished for a Director who was a little more practical.

That afternoon I did a rather brash thing. I called all the young people together, gang members, drug addicts, college boys and girls, staff members, and told them that the Center was safe.

There was a great rejoicing. 'I think we ought to go into the chapel and thank God,' I said.

So we did. We went in, closed the doors, and praised the Lord for having saved this home for His use. Finally someone looked up and asked:

'Say, David, where'd the money come from?'

'Oh, it hasn't come in yet.'

Twenty-five blank expressions. Twenty-five frozen smiles.

'It hasn't come in yet,' I went on. 'But before September 10, the money will be in our hands, I'm sure. By that date, I'll have a cheque for $15,000 to show you. I just thought we ought to thank God ahead of time.'

And with that I walked out.

September 1 came. September 2, 3, 4. I spent a great deal of time on the telephone, seeing if I could find the solution to our problem. Every sign pointed to His wanting us to continue our work. The summer had been rather successful. Our records showed that 2,500 young people all over New York had made a real contact with Love; they had turned their lives over to Christ. Hundreds of boys and girls had poured through the Center on their way to new jobs, to new outlooks, to creativity. Twelve were actually preparing for the ministry.

'And it all started with that picture in *Life*,' I said to Gwen one night as we were reviewing the year.

'Isn't it strange that you've never been allowed to see those boys from the trial?' said Gwen.

It was strange. I had written, and telephoned, and knocked on doors for nearly four years. But, for reasons beyond my comprehension, I was never allowed to work closely with the very boys whose tragedy had brought me to New York in the first place. Their fate and the fate of Israel (ex-President of the Mau Maus) remained for a while at least in the hands of the state. Perhaps, when the boys were released from prison I would be allowed to tell them about the concern that was still on my heart for their futures.

There was a boy, however, from those very first days in New York, whose life still touched mine: Angelo Morales.

One morning Angelo came to visit us. Together we relived that first day when he bumped into me on the stairs outside Luis Alvarez' father's apartment. And now Angelo himself was about to graduate from seminary. He too would be working with me at the Center.

'If there *is* a Center, Angelo,' I said, sharing with him our financial problems.

'Is there anything I can do?' Angelo asked.

'Yes. Get into the chapel with the others and pray. While you are praying, we'll be on the phone.'

Every member of our Board was busy making telephone calls to old friends of the Center. Help came in, but never in the quantity needed to meet the $15,000 note on September 10. Among the telephone calls was one to Clem Stone's office in Chicago. Harald Bredesen placed it, admitting openly that he was a little embarrassed. Clem had already been more than generous with the Center. We tried to keep him in close touch with the progress of our work at all times, not just when we needed money; but I suspect that when Clem heard a call was coming from Teen Challenge Center his natural instinct was to place a quick, protecting hand over his wallet.

It was Clem's son whom Harald reached on the telephone, September 8. They had a long talk. Harald told about the work that had been accomplished already, and he thanked the Stones for their part in that. Then, with a shrug, he finally got to the point.

'We've got to have $15,000 by the day after tomorrow,' he said, and he explained why. 'I have no idea what your position is at this moment. And I'm certainly not going to ask for a decision while you're on the telephone. But talk this over with your father. Tell him thanks for what he's already done to help. And then let's just see what happens.'

September 10 arrived.

The morning mail came. We opened it eagerly. There were envelopes from children sending in their pennies.

'Thank you, Lord,' I said. 'We couldn't do without these pennies.'

And that was all.

The morning chapel service began. Everyone was gathered, everyone prayed and sang. Here and there I heard our young people still thanking God for sending us the cheque for $15,000.

In the middle of the service, I was called to the door.

It was a Special Delivery. I looked at the postmark: Chicago, Illinois.

I opened the envelope, and inside was a certified cheque for exactly $15,000.

I couldn't talk when I took that piece of paper into the chapel. I stood before the fireplace with its sheaf of harvested wheat in bas-relief on the mantel. I couldn't talk, so I just held up my hand for silence, and when the room was quiet, Paul DiLena handed the cheque to the young boy nearest me.

'Pass that around, will you please?' Paul said, almost inaudibly.

The cancelled cheque, which Clem Stone now has in his files in Chicago, tells a mute story of the wonderful leading of

God among young people in New York City. It is properly endorsed, properly deposited. But it is more than that. If you look closely at that cheque, you will see that it is stained: it is really quite grubby from having passed through the hands of two dozen youngsters who have learned what it is to believe. And perhaps there are a few tear-stains on it, too. Tears of gratitude to a God who moves in mysterious ways His wonders to perform.

Epilogue

This story, of course, is far from finished.

Each day new chapters are being written in the transformed lives of youngsters all over New York.

But another volume is being written, too. This one is oriented to Chicago, not New York. A brand new Teen Challenge Center already exists and is in operation in that city. Borrowing on the mistakes and successes of our pilot project here, Chicago's Center is bounding ahead.

Like the home in New York, it will operate on a budget of close to $50,000 during the first year alone. And like our home here, it will operate on current balances of fourteen, fifteen, sixteen dollars at a time. When I flew out to Chicago to help get the new Center started, I could just hear echoes of Paul DiLena's question, 'Where's the money, where's the books, and who's in charge here?'

The Holy Spirit is in charge.

As long as He remains in charge, the programmes will thrive. The minute we try to do things by our own power we will fail.

This is the guiding principle of the Center here in New York; it is the principle which directs our new Center in Chicago, and the one that is starting in Philadelphia, and in Boston, and in Los Angeles, and in Toronto.

The Holy Spirit is in charge here.

We should write it for all to see on the lintels of every doorway we build. But since that might seem like so many words, we will do better: we will write it in our lives. And in all the lives we can reach out to and touch and inspire with the living Spirit of God.

We want to hear from you. Please send your comments about this book to us in care of the address below. Thank you.